D0423016

WINNING THE FIGHT BETWEEN
YOU AND YOUR DESK

Also by Jeffrey J. Mayer

If You Haven't Got the Time to Do It Right,
When Will You Find the Time Do It Over?

Find the Job You've Always Wanted in Half the Time with Half the Effort

WINNING THE FIGHT BETWEEN
YOU AND YOUR DESK

Use Your Computer to Get Organized,
Become More Productive,
and Make More Money

JEFFERY J. MAYER

HarperBusiness
A Division of HarperCollinsPublishers

HarperCollins books may be purchased for educational, business, or sales promotional use. For information, please write: Special Markets Department, HarperCollins Publishers, Inc., 10 East 53rd Street, New York, NY 10022.

FIRST EDITION

Designed by Alison Lew

Library of Congress Cataloging-in-Publication Data

Mayer, Jeffrey J.
  Winning the fight between you and your desk : use your computer to get organized, become more productive, and make more money / Jeffrey J. Mayer.
    p. cm.
  Includes index.
  ISBN 0-88730-674-8
  1. Office practice—Automation. 2. Business—Data processing. 3. Business records—Management—Data processing. 4. Time management. I. Title
HF5548.M36 1994
651.8—dc20   93-48256

94 95 96 97 98 ❖/RRD 10 9 8 7 6 5 4 3 2 1

In memory of my father,
who would have loved the computer.

Contents

■ *Part II*

Winning the Fight Between You and
Your Office   67

■ *Part IV*

Winning the Fight Between You and Your Body 205

ACKNOWLEDGMENTS

I would like to thank my wife, Mitzi, and my daughter, Delaine, for their love, support, and encouragement during the six months it took me to complete this book.

I would also like to thank my publisher, Jack McKeown, my editor, Virginia Smith, and Frank Mount for their assistance in helping me shape my ideas and turn them into this book. It was greatly appreciated.

Mr. Neat–The Clutterbuster

Let me describe a typical office. This one looks as if a tornado had gone through it. There are piles of paper everywhere. They're on the desk, the credenza, the chairs, and the floor. Next to the phone is a pile of pink phone slips. On the wall are so many Post-It notes that you could easily mistake them for a swarm of butterflies. And off in a corner are several stacks of old newspapers, magazines, and trade journals still waiting to be read. Of course, the person who works in this office *looks* busy, but there's a world of difference between being busy and being productive. Most people don't realize that a lot of time, effort, and energy is wasted looking for papers and files that are *lost* on the top of the desk.

I know all about this because I'm an executive efficiency expert. My business is helping busy people get organized so they can get more work done, in less time and with less effort. I work with a person one-on-one, in their office, and in two hours I'm able to transform a desk that looks like a toxic waste dump—with piles of paper everywhere—into something that resembles the flight deck of an aircraft carrier. By the time we're finished the only things that remain on the desk are the telephone and a pad of paper. Everything else either has been filed, passed on to someone else, or thrown away. For this I'm paid $1,000 a person.

I've been profiled by almost every major newspaper and magazine in the country—*USA Today* dubbed me "Mr. Neat, the Clutterbuster," *People* magazine called me the "Power Desk Cleaner to Corporate America," and the Chicago *Sun-Times* referred to me as the "World's Most Expensive Maid." I've also given almost a thousand radio and television interviews.

I became famous because I discovered an easy way to help people improve their productivity: Clean off the piles of papers on the desk. But the clean desk isn't the goal or objective, it's a means to an end. What people really want is to get more work done in less time, and with less effort, and the place to start is with the top of the desk. The clean desk helps them to get organized. I've found that with improved organization a person becomes more productive, saves time, and in the end is able to make more money.

Twenty years ago, when I was first starting my business career, a woman with whom I worked very closely taught me how to get organized. We started with the calendar, appointment book, and to-do lists and eventually worked our way through every drawer in my desk and every file in the filing cabinet. By the time we were finished, I was able to run my business affairs with only a telephone and a pad of paper on the top of my desk. Everything else was neatly and meticulously filed away. Interestingly enough, within a short time the housekeeping of all of my co-workers and colleagues improved.

But most important, I discovered that day in and day out I was getting more work done and doing it better because I was organized. I also discovered that being organized has big benefits in other areas of my business affairs. I got my work done on time, or even ahead of schedule, because I understood the importance of starting on a project as soon as it was assigned. I was no longer waiting until the fifty-ninth minute of the eleventh hour to get started. By starting early, I would give myself plenty of time to think about, work on, and edit my work. The objective was, and still is, to have a great finished product, not a great first draft. To say the least, I overcame the procrastination habit, and best of all, I discovered that the quality of my work got better and better.

I also learned how to focus my time and energy on the projects and tasks that were most important. These are the ones that have a big payoff. Long ago I was taught that if you're going to spend a lot of time, effort, and energy on something, do it on something that will make you some money. With this in mind I try to use my time and my energy efficiently, so I can invest them in ways that will pay big dividends.

But most of all I've learned that there is a world of difference between being busy and being productive. Over the years I've consulted with thousands of people in every conceivable business or profession and came to the realization that the person who comes in early, stays late, and works weekends isn't necessarily productive, effective, or efficient. Nine times out of ten he, or she, is just working very hard, but not very smart.

I put all of my timesaving tips, ideas, techniques, and strategies on paper when I wrote my best-selling book *If You Haven't Got the Time to Do It Right, When Will You Find the Time to Do It Over?* In it I explain, in step-by-step detail, how easy it is for a person to get organized. We start with the most common stumbling block to improving productivity—a messy desk. Most people don't realize that they're wasting thirty to sixty minutes every day looking for papers that are *lost* on the top of their desk. Simply by cleaning off the piles, and getting organized, they're able to cut at least an hour of wasted time from their workday.

Once I help a person get organized they're able to put my time-saving and productivity-improving ideas, techniques, and strategies to work. I show them that with a little planning it's easy to set priorities, focus on the tasks that are most important, and get their work done on time. In the end, the goal is to make some money and have some quality time in which to enjoy it.

A few things have changed since I wrote *If You Haven't Got the Time to Do It Right, When Will You Find the Time to Do It Over?* Yes, everybody still has a need to get organized, but many of the things we were doing with a pencil and a piece of paper can now be done electronically with a computer. In just a few short years the personal computer has become a very important part of our lives. Today the majority of us would find it impossible to get along without it. I know I sure would. I can't imagine how I could conduct my business and personal affairs, or write this book, without one. Since the birth of the IBM personal computer in 1982 the world hasn't been the same. We're in the midst of a second Industrial Revolution.

How I Became a Computer User

Like many of you, I would have to say that I'm rather new to using computers. My need for a computer evolved slowly. In the spring of 1988, I started writing what would become my first book, *If You*

Haven't Got the Time to Do It Right, When Will You Find the Time to Do It Over? When I first sat down to put my ideas on paper, all I had was a simple, old-fashioned typewriter—at least it was electric. As I would write, edit, and write some more, I quickly realized that I was writing everything over and over again. I was spending more time retyping the text that I liked, instead of rewriting the text that needed improvement. The process was so slow, cumbersome, and laborious that I was exhausted before I even got to the point where I was writing new text. At such a pace I knew that I would never complete a book.

For a time management expert, this seemed to me to be a *big* waste of valuable time. I thought that my life would be a lot easier if I was able to move text around on the page by "pasting and cutting," instead of having to retype the whole page when all I wanted to do was move a sentence from one paragraph to another.

At that point I felt a computer was too expensive and too complicated to use, so I purchased a simple word processor. It was really nothing more than a fancy typewriter with a video monitor. It had an optional disk drive that was attached by a cable and cost me almost $1,000.

I used this machine for only a few months and then realized how limited it really was. It still didn't have the features I needed to write a book. So I upgraded to a more powerful word processor, at a cost of $2,000, less a trade-in. This one had a video monitor, a built-in disk drive, and a keyboard that was detachable from the printer. I liked the machine, but there was only one problem. It printed like a typewriter, one page at a time. I thought hand-feeding the printer was a terrible waste of time, so I spent another $500 for an automatic sheet feeder. The machine got me through my first book, but just barely.

In the spring of 1991, I began work on my second book, *Find the Job You've Always Wanted, in Half the Time with Half the Effort.* I quickly came to the conclusion that the word processor didn't have the features I needed to write another manuscript. I broke down, bit the bullet, and bought a real computer, an IBM clone with a 386/16MHz chip, and a 40-megabyte hard drive. I also bought a copy of WordPerfect and purchased a laser printer. The "MHz" (megahertz) is the term used to describe the speed at which a computer processes instructions; the "386" refers to the type of computer chip that is installed inside the computer. The whole system cost just under $4,000 ($2,500 for the computer and software). I didn't want to lose the work I had already done on the word processor, so I spent an additional $425 to convert the word processing files to the WordPerfect format.

I thought I was in heaven. This new system was great. I could do so many different things. Using the many features of WordPerfect, I found writing the manuscript was easy. With time, my manuscript grew in length, and then I started using WordPerfect's Table of Contents feature. With this feature WordPerfect will create a table of contents from the document by searching for the codes that I had previously inserted within the document.

When I used the Table of Contents feature, I quickly understood what people meant when they said that a computer was slow. It took so long for the computer to create the table of contents that I thought I was watching grass grow. I lived with this machine for only six months and then bought a new memory board, a 386/33MHz, and increased my random access memory (RAM) to 4 megabytes. This cost me another $1,200, but I was happy and I finished the book.

When I began to write this book, I added software to make my computer run faster and a data compression program to double the size of my 40-megabyte hard drive, but I still didn't have enough disk space. So I added a 245-megabyte hard drive. Now I had the storage capacity I needed but was unhappy because I still felt that my machine was running too slowly. I longed for a faster computer. And then one day I looked in the newspaper and saw how low the prices for a new computer had fallen. So I traded in my old machine, kept my disk drives, monitor, and keyboard, and bought a 486/50MHz DX2. It only cost me $950 plus a trade-in.

I'm sure that many of you have had experiences similar to mine. However, I want to stress that I am not suggesting that you go out and buy a new computer this very minute, but don't be surprised if you decide to do so in the near future. But before you do, there are some inexpensive software products that I'll be discussing later in this book that are designed to increase a computer's power, speed, and disk capacity. These enhancement products will help you get more from your computer now, and when you're ready to make your purchase, I'm sure that prices will have fallen even lower.

A Computerized Appointment Book Inspired Me to Write This Book

For years I've kept an appointment book, calendar, to-do list, and name and address book, and I've always suggested to my clients that they do the same. These are the tools that keep a person organized, on track, and on time. They help them to stay on top of all their unfinished work, projects, and tasks. That's one of the reasons leather-bound personal organizers and planners have become so popular.

One day I received a complimentary copy of a computerized appointment book, calendar, and to-do list in the mail. I promptly installed it on my computer and within minutes I was talking to myself: "WOW!!! THIS IS GREAT!" I couldn't believe how easy it was to use and instantly saw how it could help me automate many of the things I had previously been doing by hand. My life hasn't been the same since.

I began buying computer magazines to learn more about this new type of software—personal information managers—and after reading about an interesting program would then visit my local software store to purchase a copy just to see how it worked. I soon discovered that there was a host of new software products specifically designed to make corporate executives, businesspeople, office workers, and entrepreneurs who work out of their homes—like me—more productive and efficient. Many of the people who were developing this software were entrepreneurs who were looking at the kinds of tasks that businesspeople and office workers were doing. Then they would write software that would allow the computer to automate the work. I spoke with one person who hated filling out expense reports, so he wrote a software program, Expense It!, that allows the computer to do it. Another felt the same way about medical claim forms, so he wrote Med$ure.

On the following pages I'm going to tell you about the newest and most powerful software programs that have recently been developed with the sole purpose and objective of making you more productive, saving you time, and helping you to make more money. If you're already using a personal computer I'm going to show you how you can use it to improve your productivity even further. And if you've never used a computer, I'm going to give you plenty of reasons why you should go out and purchase one.

Today you can use the computer to automate many of the tasks and other work activities that you have previously been doing with a pencil and a piece of paper. Because of the increased power and speed of the newer computers, the ease of using Microsoft's graphical user interface, Windows, and the new software programs, you can use the computer to do much more than just create letters, proposals, and documents with a word processor; crunch numbers with a spreadsheet program; or keep track of customers, clients, or suppliers with a database. Let me give you a brief overview of what you'll find in this book.

A Brief Overview

Part I: Winning the Fight Between You and Your Desk

We start with the most important business tools: your calendar, appointment book, to-do lists, and Rolodex file. You can now keep track of your day and your life with a computerized personal information manager instead of relying solely on a paper-based personal organizer. These computerized personal information managers are designed to help you stay on top of your appointments, your telephone calls, your long-term and short-term projects, and almost everything else that is going on in your business life.

The beauty of these programs is that they're designed to work with your personal organizers—your Day-Timer, Day Runner, Franklin Day Planner, Filofax, or any other organizer you may have become attached to. So, if you love that leather-bound book, you don't have to give it up.

In addition to helping you organize your daily activities, these programs can also help you organize all the information you have accumulated about the people in your life, and the projects and activities you're involved with. With a personal information manager's powerful search capabilities—you can find almost any piece of information in a fraction of a second—you'll quickly find that you're no longer writing notes on scraps of paper or the back of an envelope. When you have an important thought or idea, you'll store it inside your computer—where you have easy access—instead of losing it in the piles of paper on your desk.

In addition to personal information managers there are contact managers and database programs. These simple, easy-to-use contact management programs will help you to keep in touch with the people who are important to your business lives—customers, clients, or suppliers—and make sure that you stay on top of everything that is going on between you and them. And if you want to create your own contact management or information management program from scratch, there are some great and easy-to-use database programs that have just come on the market.

On the other hand, maybe you don't want, or need, the computer to look after every aspect of your life. In that case you probably don't need the power of a personal information manager. But you can certainly use a computerized name and address book. These easy-to-use programs make keeping in touch with, and keeping track of, the important people in your life a pleasure.

Part II: Winning the Fight Between You and Your Office

In Part II, I'll show you how you can use your computer to make you more efficient in your daily activities. Did you know that there are programs available where you can send and receive faxes directly from your computer? The days of standing at a fax machine are over. You write a letter in your word processor and instantly send it out as a fax. It's as simple as that. And when you receive a fax into your computer, you can edit it, annotate notes on it, save it to file, append it to another file, send it on to someone else, or print it on your laser printer. All this happens without ever handling a piece of paper.

You may wonder how you sign a letter if you're sending it directly from a computer? With an inexpensive scanner, you can make a graphic image of your signature, which you then insert into the document. Your letterhead can be scanned into the document as well.

While we're on the subject of scanners, you can now scan full documents into your computer with inexpensive, easy-to-use scanners. Attach an automatic sheet feeder, and it's just like making copies with your office copier. Once the document has been scanned, the scanned image is converted to ASCII text using a feature called optical character recognition (OCR). Once converted, you can edit the document in your word processor.

If you've ever retyped printed information into your computer, you know what a time-consuming task that is. With a scanner, the job's done in seconds. You can also scan photographs and pictures into your computer for use in your letters or presentations. This is the beginning of the creation of the paperless office.

While we're on the subject of the paperless office, many businesses have set up local area networks (LANs) that are bringing the dream of a paperless office closer to reality. LANs allow people to access files that are stored on another computer. Once the network has been created, an electronic mail (E-mail) system can be added. This allows people to send and receive messages from their computers.

With the increased popularity of LANs, it's now possible to use the network to schedule appointments and meetings with other people electronically. You can also use the computer to complete various company forms, like expense reports. In fact, there is even software that will prepare your expense reports for you. Once the form's been completed, it's sent over the network to the accounting department. These tools are fantastic time savers and paper reducers.

For those of you who need to keep track of your time, there are some powerful programs that help you keep track of how you spend every moment of your day. If you bill by the hour, this will certainly help you make more money. Or maybe you would like to discover how much time a particular project is *actually* taking you or your staff to complete.

Everybody has projects—big ones and little ones—that need to get done, and there are simple, easy-to-use project-scheduling programs designed to help you complete your projects on time and under budget. They also are designed to use Gantt charts. (A Gantt chart is a colored graph showing the many tasks that need to be done to complete a particular project. It displays the date when each task is scheduled to begin and end, and the percentage of completion of the project at any given moment in time.) And if you need to design flowcharts, or organization charts, you can use the computer to do that also.

Many people use more than one computer. They have a PC on their desk, one at home, and a notebook that they carry with them when they're out of town. Keeping information on several computers often creates a problem: You're never sure you're working on the latest version of a spreadsheet or document. Now there's a file transfer utility program that keeps all the files on all your PCs up-to-date and current. No matter which computer you're using, you'll know that you're always working on the latest version of your document or spreadsheet.

With that in mind, if you need to move information from one computer to another, there's software that will copy your files at the very fast rate of 8 megabytes per minute and transfer this information between computers via cables. This makes the task of data transfer simple, effortless, and easy. You no longer have to copy data to a floppy disk (each floppy disk holds 1.44 megabytes of data), insert the floppy into the new computer, and copy it onto the hard drive.

You can also use the computer to organize your home finances, pay your bills, and keep track of all your investment transactions. This makes the chore of writing checks much easier. Your frequently recurring expenses can be memorized, so you don't have to write the same payee's name month after month. Instead of writing your checks by hand, you run them through your printer. When it comes time to prepare your taxes, you can print a report showing the details of all your transactions or transfer your information to a tax preparation program.

If you're running a small business, you may be interested in a complete bookkeeping program that enables you to keep track of your invoices, accounts receivable, cash flow, and sales and profits. It can also write your checks, as well as keep track of your assets and liabilities, accounts receivable, and accounts payable.

Finally, one of the biggest productivity-improvement tools provided with every computer program is a macro, which is a series of recorded keystrokes. When the macro is turned on, these keystrokes are played back automatically, just like the autodial feature on your phone. With macros, you can automate many of the repetitive keyboard tasks you do over and over every day.

Part III: Winning the Fight Between You and Your Computer

In Part III, I'll talk about how you can become more productive by getting more out of your computer. We start by cleaning up your hard drive.

Clean up Your Hard Drive

Most people treat their hard drives as if they were filing cabinets with unlimited capacity. They put more and more papers (computer files and programs) in, until it's filled beyond capacity. So I suggest we clean up the hard drive. This means deleting unnecessary files, especially automatic backup files, and copying other files to floppy disks so the information can be stored in a desk drawer.

In addition to old files, we all have programs that we no longer use and that are taking up valuable disk space. You no longer have to delete these unused programs yourself. There is now software that will not only remove the old program, it will also delete the additional initialization, *.INI, files that were created. (*.INI files contain the program information that defines the Windows environment.)

Organize Your Files

You would be surprised at how much time people waste looking for files inside their computer because they can't find the file they're looking for. As files accumulate, locating a particular file quickly can become impossible. This problem is generally caused by the limitations of the DOS operating environment. You can only give a file a name using 8 characters, plus a 3-character extension.

Software has now been created that allows you to use names of up to 256 characters for each file, allowing recognizable descriptions. Furthermore, you can group your files by subject, project, or client, and place them in a single *folder*. This means that you can place all the files for a single project—letters, memos, spreadsheets, presentations, faxes, etc.—in a single file folder. There you can view each file at once, instead of going in and out of separate directories.

Expand Your Hard Drive's Capacity.

Nobody ever has enough data storage space on their hard drive because of two trends: The programs themselves are becoming more powerful, which means they are larger in size—WordPerfect 6.0 for DOS takes up 16 megabytes, and WordPerfect 5.2 for Windows takes up 12 megabytes—and everybody is using their machines to do more things, so they have more programs installed. With a data compression program, you can double the storage of your present hard drive.

There are also programs designed to increase your computer's performance. With some off-the-shelf software, you can dramatically increase your computer's memory, speed, and power.

Back up Your Work.

The most important thing a computer user should regularly do is to back up his or her work. The question is not if you will have some type of computer failure—it's only a question of when! There are two areas of concern: What happens to the information that's on the screen if your computer locks up and must be rebooted? And what would you do if there was a general failure that damaged or destroyed files on your hard drive?

Today there are some easy-to-use backup programs that have automated the task of backing up data onto floppy disks or a tape drive. And if you have a disk failure, you *must* have an emergency data recovery program that will help you to recover or restore damaged files.

Part IV: Winning the Fight Between You and Your Body

Many people who spend a lot of time sitting at a computer keyboard are beginning to suffer hand, wrist, arm, shoulder, or back injuries that are often referred to as repetitive stress injuries. This is frequently caused by the constant uninterrupted repetition of a few hand movements for hours at a time. It's important that you become aware of the symptoms, so that if you begin to feel pain or discomfort, you can treat the problem before it becomes more serious. But, most important, there are a number of things you can do to insure that you won't suffer an injury.

We'll begin with ergonomically designed chairs that are designed to reduce the stress on your lower back. Then there are user-friendly ergonomic keyboards, and computer programs that remind you to get up from your chair every hour or so and do some exercises.

We're all very concerned about our health, and there are some new programs that will help you take a more active role in managing your health, and if you're trying to watch your weight, you can use the computer to keep track of the calories you eat and the calories you burn up.

And then there's medical insurance. We are all very concerned about health care, and there's a program that will help you determine what is the best health insurance plan for you. First determine your insurance needs, then compare policies and benefits, and finally make a purchase. Should you have a medical claim, the program will track the expenses and print out the insurance claim forms.

The Best Program Is the One That Works Best for You

As I discuss these programs I'm going to explain in general terms how they work and then describe some of their unique features. I am not trying to determine which program is the "best program." That is not my goal. The best program is the one that best serves *your* needs and solves your problems.

There are a few things I want to mention right now and would like you to keep in the back of your mind as you're reading this book.

■ I don't expect you to purchase *every* piece of software that I'm discussing. I want you to read the book from cover to cover—to get an idea of the kinds of things you can have your computer do for you—and then go out and purchase the one piece of software that will have the most benefit to you today.

■ After you've used your new software for a while, you should then look through this book a second time and decide which piece of software you want to purchase next. Within the span of six months you should plan to add two or three productivity-improving software programs to your collection.

I would like to add that almost every piece of software comes with a money-back guarantee. If you're not fully satisfied with the product you can usually return it for a full refund within the first thirty days. This applies to both software purchased in a store and software that is ordered over the phone. If you are going to purchase software from a mail order company or directly from the manufacturer, make it a point to ask two questions: Does the refund include the cost of shipping and handling? Is there a restocking fee?

For convenience I'm including the name, address, and telephone number of each software manufacturer, along with the manufacturer's suggested retail price, so as to make it easy for you to get product information or to place an order. When you find a piece of software that you want to purchase, make it a point to shop around. Almost every piece of software can be purchased at a substantial discount—30 to 50 percent—from the suggested retail price.

Windows as a Productivity-Improvement Tool

The milestone event that changed the way we use the personal computer was the creation of Microsoft's Windows. But the revolution came slowly. The early versions of Windows were slow and cum-

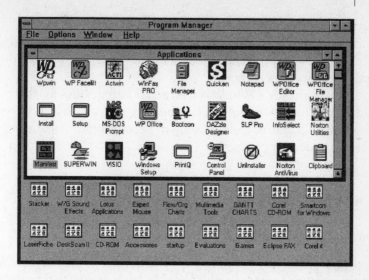

bersome, the computers weren't powerful enough, and there wasn't much software available.

Today that's not the case. With each new generation of computer chip, a piece of silicon about the size of a postage stamp, the manufacturers have discovered ways to increase the processing power and speed of the computer. Let's take a quick look at the evolution of the computer chip: In eleven years, from 1982 to 1993, we've gone from chips that had 29,000 transistors (the 286), to Intel's Pentium, which has 3,100,000 transistors. In between there was the 386 (275,000 transistors), and the 486 (1,200,000 transistors). The powerful 486 can do more than forty times the work of the 286, and four times the work of a 386. The Pentium can do two-and-a-half times the work of the 486.

With this increased computing power has come increased processing speed. Each new generation of computer has been able to perform a greater number of mathematical calculations in a shorter time than the previous generation of machines. This has given the software developers the opportunity to write newer and more powerful computer programs. In the summer of 1993 the sales of Windows software finally caught up with, and exceeded, the sales of DOS software.

The Windows operating environment provided not just an opportunity to get away from the DOS operating system by using a graphical user interface (GUI) (pronounced GOO-ey), where you use pull-down menus and icons to activate the program's commands. It created a new opportunity to take full advantage of all the power that's built into your computer.

If you're already a Windows user, you'll find the uses for this new productivity-improving software to be very exciting. If you haven't tried Windows, you're truly missing an opportunity to enhance dramatically your daily productivity.

Removing Some of the Myths of Windows

Point and Click Mouse

Having become very comfortable with the use of the keyboard, I wasn't sure that I wanted to be *forced* to use a mouse to operate my programs. Much to my delight and surprise, I discovered that you don't have to do everything with a mouse. You can execute every command by using the keyboard instead of the mouse to access the pull-down menus. To activate the pull-down menu, all you need to do is tap the ALT key and a letter, and the menu comes down. In addition, many commands allow you to use a combination of "shortcut keys" to execute a command, like to copy text: First you block the text, by holding down the SHIFT + ARROW keys, then you copy the text by pressing CONTROL + INSERT. To paste the text, you press SHIFT + INSERT. With shortcut keys, you don't even have to use the pull-down menu.

The point-and-click mouse, however, is a very important part of using Windows, and you'll quickly find that you enjoy using it. Windows even comes with a few games that are designed to help you sharpen your "mousing" skills. One of the most popular is solitaire. After playing a few games, you'll be proficient at using the click-and-drag features of the mouse.

For those of you who are concerned with the wasted time and motion that come with removing your hands from the keyboard to use the mouse, there are now keyboards available that have a trackball built in; and at least one keyboard manufacturer, Key Tronic, is designing wristrests with a trackball inside. This allows you to control the cursor with your thumb without ever taking your hands away from the keyboard.

You Can Keep All of Your DOS Programs

Just because you've installed Windows doesn't mean that you have to replace all of your favorite DOS programs with Windows applications. Many DOS programs run under Windows in just the same way they run under DOS. (I'm writing this book using both WordPerfect for DOS and WordPerfect for Windows.) But there are two very big reasons why you should run all your DOS programs under Windows: Multitasking allows your computer to run more than one program at a time, and Windows' Clipboard gives you the ability to move information from one program to another.

Doing Two Things at Once: Multitasking

Multitasking is a feature that allows you to run two or more programs at the same time. These can be either DOS programs and/or Windows programs. The process is called time-sharing. Depending upon the configuration of your computer, you may be able to run three, four, or even five programs at once, giving you several major benefits:

■ When you have more than one program running at a time, you can instantly move between programs simply by pushing a few buttons. Press the ALT + TAB keys, and you can toggle between your active programs. You're no longer forced to save your current file, close your application, open the new application, and retrieve the new file. This aspect of Windows is all by itself a fabulous productivity-improvement tool. In doing my software analysis, I always had several programs running at once. I would test a feature in one program to see how it worked, then I would test the same feature in a second program, and when I was finished I would toggle over to WordPerfect and write about it.

■ You have several options available to you as to how you want to view your different programs. You can have the program take up the entire screen or just a portion of it. If you choose to use just a portion of your screen with the current program, you can then see all the other programs at the same time. With a click of the mouse, you can easily move any of these programs to the foreground. You can even resize each screen, enabling you to look at a document in your word processor, as well as a spreadsheet, database, or any other program on the same screen at the same time—I did this often.

■ Another huge productivity-improvement tool of Windows is that it allows your computer to do work on one program in the background while you're doing something on another program in the foreground. Typically, if you want to sort a database, crunch numbers in your spreadsheet, or print a long document in your word processor, this would tie up your computer until this task has been completed. You may look at this "down time" as an opportunity to take a coffee break, but you're really losing productive work time. With multitasking, your computer can do this work in the background while you're doing something else in the foreground. Your computer is now accomplishing two or even three tasks at the same time. Windows allows you to improve your computer's productivity—and your own!

With the Clipboard You Can Move Information from One Program to Another

Another powerful feature of Windows is that it allows you to move information easily between different programs. Before Windows, if you wanted to move information from one program to another, you were usually forced to retype the information. With the Windows Clipboard, you can do it electronically. You copy the information in your program to the Windows Clipboard, where it provides temporary storage, and then paste it into your other program, much the same way you cut and paste words, sentences, and paragraphs within your word processor. The transfer is done in a fraction of a second.

This can even be done between DOS applications. You can transfer information from DOS to DOS, DOS to Windows, Windows to DOS, and Windows to Windows. You can even copy the contents of an entire screen. Press ALT + PRINT SCREEN, and a "snapshot" of the screen will be placed as an image onto the Clipboard, which can then be pasted into another application. That is how I got the "pictures" of the different Windows applications into this book.

I would take a snapshot of a screen and import it into WordPerfect as a graphic image. Then I *printed* the image to file, instead of *saving* it to file, using one of the Windows printer drivers, the Linotronic 330. The Linotronic 330 is a special graphics printer that prints at 1,200 dpi (dots per inch). When I had created six or seven images I would copy the Linotronic print files to a floppy disk and take it to a graphics printer who printed my images as camera ready artwork.

Windows Allows Your Programs to Share Information

Object Linking and Embedding

Object linking and embedding (OLE) allows you to transfer, share, and combine information created in different Windows applications in a powerful new way. All your different programs can now work together as teammates instead of as individual, unrelated programs. You can now create a document in your word processor that includes charts, graphics, or spreadsheets that were created in other applications and edit those charts, graphics, or spreadsheets from within your word processor.

For example, suppose you were working on a presentation in WordPerfect and decided that you needed to update the spreadsheet that had been imported from Lotus 1-2-3. With OLE, you click on the spreadsheet from within WordPerfect, and OLE launches Lotus. Then it opens the spreadsheet's file, where you can make your changes. When you're finished editing the spreadsheet and exit Lotus, you return to WordPerfect, and the changes you made in the spreadsheet are reflected in your document.

You can also add *sound* to your documents. With a sound card, which I'll discuss later, you can record music or your own voice and attach it to your document by inserting a sound icon. When you click on the icon, the recording, which can also be edited, is played back. This is a great way to make notes to yourself. When you've a thought you want to attach to your document, you speak into the microphone instead of typing it onto your document.

Dynamic Data Exchange

Dynamic data exchange (DDE) links allow you to automatically update information between two applications. Unlike OLE, you cannot edit an object from within the application that has the link. Referring to my previous illustration, if you wanted to make changes to the spreadsheet, you would have to start Lotus, open the spreadsheet file, and make your changes. But since Lotus and WordPerfect are sharing a DDE link, the changes in the spreadsheet will be displayed in the WordPerfect document. The great advantage of using dynamic data exchange is that it allows you to keep both files up-to-date and current. Whenever the spreadsheet changes, those changes will automatically be made in the word processing document.

Windows Software Programs Are Designed to Work Together

Windows offers an operating environment where all your applications use the same layouts and features. Once you have learned how to navigate within one Windows application, you'll find that every other application works basically the same.

With this in mind, many of today's new software programs are designed to work in harmony with one another. Fax programs work with word processors, which work with spreadsheets and personal information managers. You're no longer using several different types of software applications—word processor, spreadsheet, and database programs. Instead you're using your computer to create a complete and total productivity-improvement environment. Your software has become an integrated group of productivity-enhancement tools that are designed to work together seamlessly. This allows you to spend more time doing your work and less time trying to navigate your way through your computer.

Windows. Microsoft Corporation, One Microsoft Way, Redmond, WA 98052; 800-426-9400. Suggested retail price: $149.95.

Part I

WINNING THE FIGHT BETWEEN YOU AND YOUR DESK

How Do You Take Control of Your Day?

For years we've all been keeping track of our unfinished work by using daily planning books—Day-Timers, Day Runners, Filofaxes, and Franklin Day Planners—to keep track of our meetings, appointments, and to-do's. These leather-bound personal organizers are wonderful productivity-improvement tools. They help us set our priorities, organize and coordinate our important long-term projects, keep track of delegated work, and establish and set our goals. We also use them to jot down notes or background information about a meeting or phone conversations, keep track of miscellaneous ideas and thoughts, and record our tax-deductible or reimbursable expenses.

In addition to keeping track of what we need to do and when we need to do it, these personal organizers have sections that are designed to keep track of all the people with whom we're doing these things. The phone book section keeps the names, addresses, and phone numbers of our family, friends, customers, clients, and other important people.

We use these books not only to keep track of our daily activities but also to keep our lives in order. For some of us, these books play such an important role in our lives that we won't go anyplace without them. We even use them to carry our checkbooks and credit cards.

Personal Organizers Do Have Limitations

There are, however, some limitations to using a personal organizer, based upon the simple fact that you're using a pencil and paper. The same information needs to be rewritten over and over again. Let me give you a few examples.

It's Not Easy to Keep Your To-Do List Up-to-Date

Most of us keep to-do lists. We write down the names of various tasks, or other items of business that need to be done. This list is usually written on a specific day's page in a book. But what happens to that item if it isn't done on the day it was entered? You must move this item to a future day by rewriting it. If it's not moved forward, you'll find yourself constantly flipping back and forth in your book, looking for items of unfinished business. This increases the probability that you'll lose track of it. With this type of follow-up method, something important always slips through the cracks.

And if you do meticulously move your unfinished work forward, at the very least it's a time-consuming process to rewrite the same list of information from Monday's page to Wednesday's page. In reality, this is busywork, not productive work. It's almost the same as rewriting your to-do list every morning so the most important item of business is at the top of the list.

A computerized appointment book-calendar solves this problem because an unfinished task is automatically moved forward at the beginning of each day. Every unfinished task on Monday's list will automatically be moved forward, sorted by priority, and appear on Tuesday's list.

Moving or Changing To-Do Items Can Be a Lot of Work

Now what if you have the following to-do item: Call Sam Smith to set up a luncheon appointment. It's quite likely you'll have to move this item around several times because you won't be able to schedule the appointment the first time you call: On Monday, you call and learn that he's in meetings all day. When you call on Tuesday, you discover that he's out of the office till Friday. On Friday, you finally get through and set up your meeting for the following Wednesday. But late Tuesday afternoon, you get a call from Sam's assistant telling you that he's been called out of town and will need to reschedule. She asks if Thursday of the following week will be okay?

Now look at what you did physically to schedule this appointment. You first wrote down the item: Call Sam Smith to set up a luncheon appointment. Then you rewrote it when you moved it to Tuesday and rewrote it a third time when you moved it to Friday. When you scheduled the appointment, you then made an entry in your appointment book and crossed off the item on your to-do list. But when the appointment was rescheduled, you had to remove the item from Wednesday's page in your appointment book, by either erasure or by scratching it out, and rewrite the information on next Thursday's page. If the appointment had not been rescheduled, you would have had to make a new notation on your to-do list and start the whole process over again.

The computer can automate this task for you. Enter the item on your to-do list once, and you don't have to write it a second time. The program simply moves it electronically from one day to the next and from your to-do list to your appointment calendar, all with the click of a button.

Do You Like to Carry Your Calendar Around with You?

Many people have more than one calendar. They keep a calendar on their desk and carry a pocket calendar with them when they travel or are out of the office. Often, a third calendar is also kept by a secretary or administrative assistant so appointments or meetings can be scheduled while the person is away from the office.

But when a person keeps more than one calendar, eventually he or she is going to experience scheduling problems. Appointments will be written in one book that won't get into the other. This creates conflicts because he or she is supposed to be in two places, or cities, at the same time. When you keep more than one calendar, you're going to have some problems. To paraphrase an old Chinese proverb: He who has two calendars never knows his true appointment schedule.

A computerized calendar guarantees that you'll always have a true picture of your daily activities—appointments and to-do list— because it's always up-to-date. Your assistant can have a printed copy of it on his or her desk. When you leave the office, you take a printed copy with you. I'll talk about the printing capabilities of these programs a little bit later. If your assistant has access to your computer, he or she can make changes to your calendar. If you're on a network, he or she can access your calendar from his or her own computer.

It Takes a Lot of Effort to Keep Track of the People in Your Life

In today's fast-paced world, it's not easy to keep a person's vital information up-to-date. Everybody has a direct phone number and fax number. Then there's a number for the beeper, the car phone, mobile telephone, and home phone. To make this record keeping more complicated, most people will probably change jobs, positions, cities, or just phone numbers every few years, which means you constantly need to update the information. How do you do it?

Rolodex Cards Become Unreadable

In a perfect world you would rewrite the new information on a new Rolodex card, but who has the time? Instead, you just scratch out the old number and write in the new one. Soon you are left with an entry that's illegible. It doesn't take very long for the entire Rolodex card file to become unreadable and unmanageable.

Name and Address Books Get Messy

A name and address book can be even worse. You write all these handwritten names, addresses, and phone numbers on the pages of a bound book. After a couple of months of continual use, they get pretty beat-up and messy—everything in the book has been scratched out and rewritten. The pages start to tear at the binding, and the edges are wearing out from daily use. With time even the names and numbers become not only illegible, they're also impossible to locate. It doesn't take very long before you've got a really big mess. Furthermore, there's no way to delete the names of people who are no longer important to you.

What Do You Do with Business Cards?

Many of us collect business cards because we think these people may be of help to us in the future. We've all been told that good contacts are the most important things to have in business. So how do we store these names? We throw them in the lap drawer of our desk, group them together with rubber bands, or use a business card file or holder. But none of these options really helps us find and locate a name when we need it. With time, we probably won't even remember who the person is, what they do, where we met, or why we even kept the card.

Unless these cards are stored in an organized way, it's almost impossible to put them to good use. The computer offers a better alternative for keeping this information because of its much larger storage capacity, the ease with which you can edit or add new information, and the ability to find people quickly with the search features.

Put Your Personal Organizer Inside Your Computer

If you would really like to improve your daily productivity and take control of your telephone calls, to-do's, meetings and appointments, and other activities, put your personal organizer inside your computer. The whole idea of using a computer is to let you get more work done in less time. With a personal information manager, you can coordinate the basic components of your organizer—your calendar, appointment book, to-do list, and name and address book—into a single program where all the components work together in harmony.

Personal Information Managers Work with Your Personal Organizer

Personal information managers are designed to work with your personal organizer. You can have the best of both worlds: A computer program that will keep you on top of everything and a printed copy of your calendar, appointment book, to-do list, and telephone directory that you can put inside your personal organizer and take with you. You can print in any of the Day-Timer, Day Runner, Franklin Day Planner, Filofax, or other popular personal organizer page formats. In

addition, you can print your address book to any number of prefor-
matted label sizes, Rolodex cards, or envelopes. If you order blank
pages from your favorite appointment book publisher, you can run
them through your printer and then insert the pages into your book.

Franklin Day Planner and Day Runner have already come out
with computerized versions of their personal organizers. Day-Timer
has begun offering a program for PCs (it came out too late to be
included in this book) and offers a computerized calendar for the
users of pen-based computers.

Automate Your Work with a Personal Information Manager

On the following pages I'm going to tell you about some different
approaches to computerized personal information management.
Everything that you're now doing with a pencil and a piece of paper
can easily be done with one of these computer programs. All the
commands can be done with either a point-and-click mouse or from
the keyboard.

But before you go out and purchase a personal information manager, however, think about your work habits and work style. You
want to match your needs with the program's major strengths. Spend
a few minutes thinking about how you use your day book, calendar,
to-do list, and telephone calls. Also think about how you process the
papers that cross your desk and how you handle your follow-ups.
During the course of a normal business day:

- Do you schedule a lot of appointments with many different people?
- Do you have a lot of follow-up work to do?
- Do you have many joint projects with other people?
- Do you need to keep detailed notes of your telephone conversations and face-to-face meetings?
- Do you spend a lot of time on the phone?
- Do you send out a lot of correspondence?

Depending on how you work, you should look for a program that is strongest in the specific areas where you devote the majority of your time and energy.

All of these programs are easy to learn, flexible, and fun to use. Once installed, you can be up and running within minutes. The following is a basic summary of the common features of a personal information manager.

Maintain a To-Do List

The tasks on your to-do list form the core of your weekly and long-range planning. Your to-do list will help you keep track of what you have to do and when you have to do it. You can enter as many tasks as you like. The more tasks you include, the more control you have over everything that is going on in your business and personal life. New tasks can easily be added, completed tasks can be crossed off, and things you decide that you aren't going to do can be deleted. Unfinished to-do's are automatically moved to the following day.

When you enter a task on your to-do list, you can include both a start date and a due date. An alarm can be set that will remind you to do a specific task at a certain time. You can prioritize your tasks, and each day the personal information manager will sort the list. When a task is completed, a check is placed in the status box or a line is drawn through the item.

Think back to the example of scheduling lunch with Sam Smith. Let's change the situation a bit. When you reached him on Friday, suppose he said that he would be going out of town for a few days next week and suggested you give him a call a week from Monday, on the twenty-first. With your personal information manager, you can move the phone call from Friday to Monday, the twenty-first, with a couple of clicks with your mouse. When Monday comes, this call to Sam Smith will be displayed at the top of your to-do list. If you want, you can append a note to the phone call that says something like: "Sam said to call on the twenty-first." The date you typed the note will be automatically inserted in the note. When you call Sam and schedule the appointment for

Thursday, the twenty-fourth, you click on the to-do item with your mouse, move it to 12:00 noon on the twenty-fourth, click the mouse again, and you've scheduled your appointment.

Recurring tasks can also be added to your task list. If you've got to prepare for a staff meeting every Monday morning, you could have a recurring to-do item that appears every Thursday or Friday. If you've got to do the payroll the fifteenth and thirtieth of every month, you could have a to-do item appear as a reminder on the fourteenth, and twenty-ninth of every month.

To-do items that aren't very important at the moment or don't demand your immediate attention, but that you don't want to forget, can be moved forward to a future day when they will become a more active item.

You'll Never Lose Track of a Phone Call

We all spend hours of our valuable time on the telephone every day. Keeping track of all these incoming and outgoing calls is easy with a personal information manager. Some programs are designed with a separate list for things to do and another for telephone calls; others combine the two. Either way, keeping track of telephone calls is essentially the same as taking care of any other business item that would be on your to-do list.

But look at what a personal information manager can do for you. When you need to make a call, the personal information manager will dial the phone. With the timer, you can keep track of the length of the call. And you can keep a record of who you spoke to as well as the purpose of the conversation. This *phone log* is a perfect tool for quick reference and is especially good for maintaining accurate billing records. You can also append notes to the call so you can have a more detailed description of what you discussed. You can keep a log for both incoming and outgoing calls, which can also be printed as a report.

The phone log also helps manage the task of staying on top of all your calls because you can keep a record of the status of each and every one. This helps you to take complete control over all your telephone activities. At a glance you can see which are calls you must return, which are calls that you must make again because the person wasn't in, and which are calls where you left a message and are expecting them to call you later.

Scheduling Appointments Is a Breeze

When you schedule appointments, you not only select the time that your appointment or meeting is to begin, but you also can enter an ending time, so you have an idea as to how long this particular meeting is supposed to take. An alarm can also be set to remind you that the meeting is coming up. (You can choose to have different kinds of reminders, in addition to the traditional beep. You can select Bach, Beethoven, Christmas carols, or the 1812 Overture.) Notes can also be appended to each entry in your schedule as a reminder of the purpose or nature of the meeting.

You can view your calendar in several formats. You can look at a single day, a week at a glance, or a month at a time. When you need to schedule a business trip or vacation weeks or months in the future, this gives you the flexibility to look for blocks of time.

Recurring events, like your Monday morning staff meeting or Wednesday evening tennis game, need only be entered once. Thereafter the recurring event will be permanently added to your schedule. Special days like birthdays, anniversaries, office or family events that you want to be reminded of, can also be added to the calendar. With this feature, you'll never miss an important birthday or anniversary because the item is carried forward year after year.

Keeping in Touch with Everybody Is Easy

Personal information managers are designed to help you keep in touch with everybody in both your professional and personal lives. Some programs format their directory like a phone book; others look like the cards in a Rolodex file. All of them help you keep your important information about your contacts at your fingertips. The directories have space for several different phone numbers (home, work, fax, car, mobile, 800 number, etc.), and you can group each name into different categories— customer, client, prospect, business, personal, etc.—if you want to use the mail merge features and send the same letter to a group of people.

Entries in the appointment book or to-do list are linked to the name and address book. Click on the entry in your appointment book, and the entry in the phone book will appear. This makes contact management easier. Information in the address book, like a name, address, and greeting, can be imported into your word processor when you want to send a letter. This feature makes sending letters a breeze.

Improve Your Memory with the Notepad

The notepad allows you to keep a detailed case history of everything that is going on in your life. You can record notes of your meetings, conversations, or your thoughts and append them to a person's record. Whenever you plan to meet with them or talk on the phone, you can review their entire case history in a matter of moments. If they happen to be calling you, you can pull up the information on the screen in an instant and refresh your memory.

Printing: You Can Take It with You

You can print information from any part of your personal information manager—appointment book, to-do list, phone book—on a variety of paper layouts. Would you like to see a list of your appointments and to-do's for tomorrow, or would you prefer to look at everything you've got scheduled for the next month?

As long as you're printing your appointments and to-do's, why not print your whole telephone directory so you've got all your important phone numbers with you. You can also print mailing labels, envelopes, and/or Rolodex cards. Each program comes with predefined page layouts—or you can create your own.

Share Your Information with Your Other Programs

If you've already got a list of names and addresses in a database, word processing merge file, or another personal information manager, you can *import* these names and addresses into the new personal information manager. You don't have to spend hours of time retyping information that you already have. And once you've created your name and address book, these records can be *exported* to other databases, spreadsheet applications, or word processing programs.

Share Your Calendar with Your Co-workers

Many of the programs allow users on a local area network (LAN) to share their calendars with other users. This is especially useful if you need to schedule group meetings. With this feature you can view the appointment calendars of other users on your network and tell them that you want to add an appointment to their schedule. You can also look for vacant time slots for a group of people when you need to schedule a group meeting.

Personal Information Managers for Windows

Lotus Organizer

When you open the Lotus Organizer you see a colored, tabbed notebook that looks just like the personal organizer you've been using for years. There are six tabbed sections—Calendar, To-Do, Address, Notepad, Planner, and Anniversary. Each section is easily customized, and all are designed to work together to help you organize your schedule, prioritize your tasks, keep in contact with your clients, and make you more productive.

To make Organizer easier to use, you execute all the commands by clicking them on from a palette of icons (small symbols) that are displayed on the screen. You can also use the pull-down menus. If you prefer to use the keyboard, Organizer provides a long list of Windows keyboard shortcuts available to you by using the CONTROL keys in conjunction with a letter on the keyboard. For example, CONTROL + T means go to today's date in the Calendar.

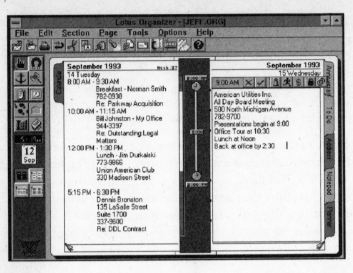

Calendar

You can look at the pages of your Calendar in one of several ways: One day at a time (per page), one week at a time (spread over two facing pages), or two weeks at a time, one week on each page. You use the Calendar section to manage your time and schedule your appointments. When you schedule an appointment, you set both the starting and ending time for your appointment using the Time Tracker. Information stored in other sections of Organizer can be linked to the Calendar section.

To-Do

The To-Do section forms the core of your weekly and long-range planning. Though the To-Do section is separate from the Appointment section, you can create a link between the sections that will display your To-Do tasks in your Calendar and allow you to edit your To-Do items from within the Calendar section.

If you have many projects, you can create additional To-Do sections for each project on which you may be working. Or maybe you just want a separate To-Do list for business items and one for personal items. You can set priorities for each task, and the status of each task is automatically color coded: Green—current; red—overdue; and blue—future.

One of the things that makes Organizer fun to use happens when an item is deleted. You click on the item, drag it across the page, and drop it into a trash can. Once inside the trash can, it bursts into flames.

You can use Calendar to launch a particular application at a preset time, like running a spreadsheet in preparation for a meeting. In Calendar, you can display entries from the To-Do, Planner, and Anniversary sections to give you a view of all your daily commitments.

Address

Organizer has a very basic name and address book for names, addresses, and phone numbers, and where you can record brief notes. This information can be cross-referenced to both the Calendar and the To-Do list. You can use the auto dialer to make calls and keep track of the call in the call log. You can create additional address books. Perhaps you want to keep an address section for your business contacts and another for your family and friends.

Notepad

You can use the Notepad section to keep notes, lists, reminders, memos, or anything you would usually write on a piece of paper. Using dynamic data exchange (DDE), you can display diagrams, organizational charts, maps, logos, spreadsheets, charts, and/or pictures. You can also use the Notepad section to build complete books of information that are specific to your work. For example, you could create a corporate manual of policies and procedures for your employees or a notebook that contains your business goals and strategies.

Organizer will automatically build a table of contents as you add more pages to Notepad. You can customize Organizer by adding new Notepad sections. Organizer's cross-referencing links allow you to link information within the same Notepad or to entries in the Appointment or To-Do sections. You can insert a time and/or date into any Notepad entry.

Planner

You can track events in the Planner. The Planner's charts look just like your wall chart where you mark events, tasks, or milestones with color-coded blocks or strips. The Planner helps you schedule and prepare for important events, such as meetings or conferences, that happen later in the year or in future years. It's especially useful if you need to designate blocks of time for a particular activity such as a vacation, an off-site meeting, or a conference.

The Planner and Calendar work together to help you manage your time. You can view Planner events when looking at your Calendar, and vice versa. This allows you to see your upcoming commitments in the context of your daily work.

Anniversary

You can use the Anniversary section to keep a list of all the important dates that you need to remember every year, such as birthdays and wedding anniversaries. After you've entered a date, that date will automatically carry forward into future years.

Lotus Organizer. Lotus Development Corporation, 55 Cambridge Parkway, Cambridge, MA 02142; 800-343-5414. Suggested retail price: $149.

Ascend

If you've been using the Franklin Day Planner, you'll love Ascend. Ascend is a highly structured personal information manager that is based on the same themes as the Franklin Day Planner. Ascend's twelve separate modules are designed to help you plan and achieve the goals that are important to you.

Values and Goals

The first step in the Ascend program is to identify your Governing Values, those principles that are most important to you. From

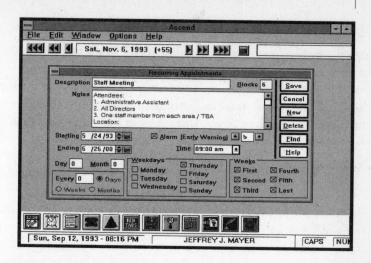

there you formulate your long-range goals, your intermediate goals, and finally your daily tasks. The publishers of Ascend believe that converting your Governing Values into goals is what gives you the power to be in control of your life and lets you spend your time doing what is *really* important to you. This process helps you to translate your values into action.

You start your Ascend day with a period of Planning and Solitude, where you give yourself a quiet, uninterrupted period of time, usually fifteen minutes, to plan your day. The first thing you do is review your Governing Values because it helps you remember what is most important. Then you review yesterday's task list one item at a time. This helps you to reselect and reassess your priorities as you move forward the tasks that you were unable to complete yesterday to today or other days in the future. This way you won't let anything slip through the cracks. Then you review your schedule for today and tomorrow to determine how much time you actually have to work on your task list. If you have scheduled appointments that will need some advance preparation, you must schedule this work into your day. This detailed process allows you to focus on the task of planning your daily activities and helps you analyze and evaluate what needs to be done.

Appointment Schedule

Ascend uses blocks of fifteen minutes to illustrate graphically how your time is being utilized throughout the day. When scheduling an appointment, you can attach a note to it as well as the person's address and telephone number. Both can be shown on the monthly planner when it is printed out. An alarm can be set as a reminder for each meeting.

Prioritized Daily Task List

With Ascend you prioritize every item on your to-do list and then rank them by order of importance. Notes can be kept for each task, enabling you to keep track of large or complicated projects. You can link tasks to a contact in your Address book to aid in keeping a detailed contact history. Tasks can be quickly forwarded, with any accompanying notes, to a future date via a pop-up calendar. Tasks can be printed in their prioritized order, including appended notes, right on the pages of your Franklin Day Planner. The Timers feature helps you keep track of how long a task actually takes to complete.

Master Task List

The Master Task List is a powerful tool for keeping track of those innumerable projects that you must accomplish sometime in the future. It serves as a temporary storage list for tasks that are important enough for you to keep around but for which you do not have time in the next couple of days—or even weeks or months!

Names, Addresses, and Phone Numbers

Ascend allows you to keep detailed information about people by providing space for five different phone numbers (home, work, fax, mobile, toll free). Each entry can be categorized (business, personal, etc.) or coded by key words. This makes it easy for you to do a search when you want to send a mailing to a select group.

Favorite Quotes

You can create a database of your favorite quotes, which can be categorized by author or key words. A favorite quote can be displayed and/or printed every time you start Ascend.

The Journal

The Journal is a *blank page* that was created for you to write your personal thoughts, feelings, evaluations, etc., daily. The Journal can be used like a personal diary to help you take a daily inventory of your personal progress and to record your thoughts and impressions of important or special events that are taking place in your life.

Printing

Ascend is designed to print on any size Franklin Day Planner page. This allows you to take a printed copy of all your important information—appointments, to-do list, telephone directory, favorite quotes—with you whenever you're away from your office.

Ascend. Franklin Quest Company, 220 West Parkway Boulevard, Salt Lake City, UT 84119; 800-654-1775. Suggested retail price: $149.

YourWay

YourWay is designed to help you organize your time, manage projects, and keep in touch with the people who are important to you. It offers a great deal of flexibility so that it will adapt to your way of working.

There are three components to YourWay: the Cardfile, the Daily Task Manager, and the Calendar.

Cardfile

The Cardfile looks like a set of three-by-five-inch Rolodex cards sitting on a tray. It is easy to use and offers a lot of flexibility because you can customize each field in the Cardfile (name, com-

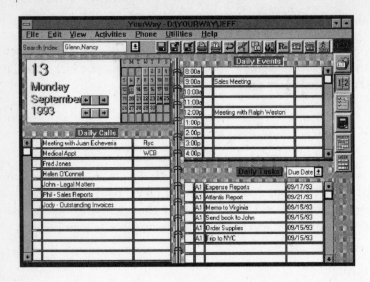

pany, address, etc.) to your own individual format. You can select what information you would like to include for a person, and in what sequence you would like to view it. Another big plus is that it automatically shares information with the Calendar/Task Manager.

Viewing information about people in your Cardfile is just like using the Rolodex cardfile on your desktop—except it's easier! With the click of a button, you move the card you want to the front of the stack. All the information about the person is right in front of you.

Each card has a pop-up notepad attached to it that will store about ten pages of information. This will help you easily maintain a contact history. The notepad also keeps track of calls that you made with the AutoDial feature, answered calls, and letters that were written through your Windows word processor.

Daily Task Manager

The Daily Task Manager allows you to view the arrangement of your tasks in different easy-to-change layouts. You can view your tasks by priority, person to whom the task was assigned, due date, date entered, or other previously defined categories (administrative, budget, marketing, etc.).

Calendar

You can view your appointment calendar in any one of several familiar formats: daily, weekly, or month-at-a-glance. The ability to change your views makes it easy for you to keep track of your time, your calls, and your commitments. You can see blocked-out meeting and appointment times at a glance and recognize and resolve scheduling conflicts easily and quickly.

Exporting YourWay Cardfile to a Database

If you want to view YourWay's data in a table format, you can export your Cardfile to a Windows database application. This will allow you to sort your information by a particular field, or you can modify the fields in all the records at one time.

Dialing the Telephone

AutoDial is a convenient, practical part of YourWay's time-management strategy. Click on the AutoDial dialogue box, and the phone number will be highlighted. When you place the call, the date, time, and length of the call will be added to the card's note. All you have to do is jot down the purpose of the conversation. When you answer a call, you can click on a dialogue box, where you enter the name of the person you're speaking with and the nature of the call. YourWay will keep track of the length of the call. This information will also be stamped to your note card.

With the Call Management feature, you can take complete control of all your telephone contacts. This allows you to keep a list of your planned calls and always know the status of each one, whether it be call back, left message, left message on voice mail, will call back, etc.

YourWay offers a completely integrated time and contact management program. YourWay includes a Quick Menu Icon, which lets you instantly access the program from any Windows application. To simplify correspondence, YourWay comes with special macros that transfer addresses and other information from YourWay to Word for Windows, WordPerfect for Windows, and Ami Pro.

All of the components of YourWay are designed to work together to help you save time and become more productive. When you jot down a note to call someone on a certain day, YourWay automatically puts a reminder in your calendar. When you use the AutoDial feature to make the call, YourWay automatically logs the call on your contact's personal note. What more can you ask for? YourWay helps you to stay on top of all your work throughout the day, every day.

YourWay. Prisma Software Corporation, 2301 Clay Street, Cedar Falls, IA 50613; 800-437-2685. Suggested retail price: $99.

Office Accelerator

Office Accelerator is designed to import names and addresses from its phone and address book directly into your Windows word processor. The beauty of Office Accelerator is how it seamlessly integrates its functions with WordPerfect for Windows, Word for Windows, or Ami Pro.

When you want to write a letter, send a fax, or print an envelope, you just select the specific item you want from the Office Accelerator menu that is displayed within your word processor, and

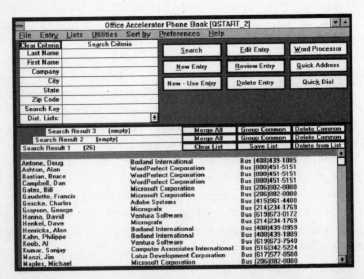

the Office Accelerator phone book appears. You select the person to whom you wish to send the correspondence, and Office Accelerator formats your letter instantly. Everything is automatically imported into your word processor and inserted into your letter: The date, the recipient's name and address, the salutation, and the closing. Office Accelerator allows you to select how each of these items will appear. When you want to send a fax, Office Accelerator will create the fax cover sheet and instruct your fax software to send the fax.

The key features of Office Accelerator are its phone and address book and its search capabilities, which will allow you to find anyone in a fraction of a second. Each phone book entry allows you to store a wide range of information: up to ten telephone numbers and ten addresses per person. The free-form note section can hold more than twenty pages of notes for each entry.

When printing envelopes, you can create and print different sizes and styles of envelopes quickly and easily. You can include your name and return address, and special notes: First class, urgent, certified, etc., giving you more than two dozen choices. You can also set up your envelopes to conform to postal regulations. They will then be formatted with a sans serif font, use uppercase letters, and eliminate all punctuation.

If you send out a lot of letters or other correspondence, Office Accelerator can be a wonderful timesaving tool. Once the basic information is entered into the phone book, you'll never have to format a letter or envelope again.

Office Accelerator. Baseline Data Systems, Inc., 3625 Del Amo Boulevard Suite 245, Torrance, CA 90503; 800-429-5325. Suggested retail price: $69.95.

Calendar Creator Plus

Have you ever thought of a calendar as a form of communication? With Calendar Creator Plus you can create a calendar that says something about you and about the events with which you're involved. You can combine colors, graphics, scanned pictures and photographs, headers, footers, and different sizes and styles of fonts

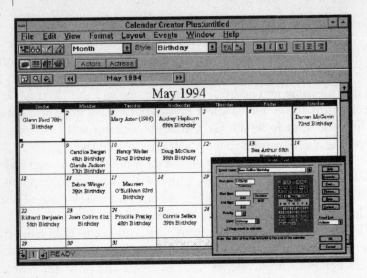

to establish a theme. To make certain events stand out, you can use different shadings of gray, reverse type—white type against a black background—and banners to highlight events that span several days.

Calendar Creator Plus is an alternative to keeping a traditional calendar. It offers you the opportunity to create distinctive calendars that have eye-catching custom results and grab people's attention.

You can use Calendar Creator Plus to keep track of your to-do lists, appointments, and meetings. When you enter a to-do item, you can give it a priority and append a note—an additional description, comment, or reminder.

Add a Picture

Pictures can make your calendar more lively and interesting. They can also convey additional information about events. Calendar Creator Plus comes with a wide selection of over three hundred clip art images grouped in such categories as business, holidays, and sports that you can use to decorate your calendars. Additional images can be imported from other programs.

Add a Banner

A banner is a long narrow box containing one line of text. If the calendar item—a vacation or business trip—goes for several days, the box will extend across all the date boxes in the calendar, starting on the day you leave and ending on the day you return.

Create a Title

You can add, modify, or create a title, subtitle, or footer to a calendar. You can also modify the font options for the days of the week, the days of the month, and the time of day.

Select Your Calendar Layout

Calendar Creator Plus has more than twenty different calendar formats: daily, weekly, multiweek, monthly, multimonth, and annual formats.

Printing Your Calendar

You can print a portrait, landscape, or double-sided calendar. You can spread a single calendar over two facing pages or print two or three calendars on the same page. You can print to any paper size, including pages that will fit into your favorite personal organizer.

Calendar Creator Plus. Spinnaker Software Corporation, 201 Broadway, Cambridge, MA 02139; 800-851-2917. Suggested retail price: $59.95.

Info Select

All of us have miscellaneous bits and pieces of random information that we need to keep. Some of it is for the long term, and others may be for only a few hours. This information is usually written on a piece of scratch paper, the back of an envelope, or a Post-It note. Within minutes, it gets buried in a pile and is forgotten. There's a pretty good

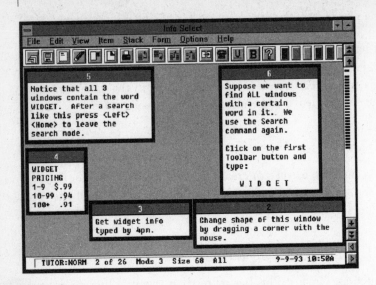

chance that we won't find it when we need it. In fact, there's a very high probability that we'll never find it again.

Info Select offers a unique solution to this problem. This personal information manager is designed to let you write your thoughts, notes, and ideas inside your computer instead of on scraps of paper. The beauty of Info Select is its search feature. You press the letter G for get, start typing a name, key word, or phrase, and the program searches for letter combinations as you're typing. When a match is found, the information pops up on the screen. You're no longer wasting valuable time searching for any piece of information that was previously buried somewhere in a pile on your desk.

I've found this to be a wonderful way to keep a telephone directory or list of miscellaneous names and numbers. When I need to schedule an appointment to get my hair cut, I just start typing *haircut*, and by the time I've typed *hai*, the name and number of my stylist appear. If the car needs service, I type *car*, and I've got the name of my mechanic. To call my editor, Virginia Smith, at HarperCollins, I type *vir*. Once the name and number appear, I push a couple of buttons, and Info Select dials the number for me. All I've got to do is pick up the phone.

Info Select makes it easy for you to keep written records of your conversations or notes to yourself. If you're running Windows, you can keep Info Select running in the background. When you have something to write down or a telephone call to make, you just "toggle" to Info Select. Once you write your thought or idea down or make your call, you go back to your work.

Info Select also has a "tickler" system so you can keep track of all your activities, or deadlines, without missing a single one and a "mail merge feature" that enables you to create personalized mailings, letters or labels, by combining form letters with address data. And you can transfer data between Info Select and other programs with both Windows and DOS versions.

Info Select is an information management tool designed to help you think. It quickly allows you to find the information you need, so you spend more of your valuable time making decisions and less of your time looking for the information you need to make that decision.

Info Select. Micro Logic Corp., P. O. Box 70, Hackensack, NJ 07602; 800-342-5930. Suggested retail price: $149.95.

Put Your Appointment Book on Your Network

Is your work group using a local area network to share messages? If so, would you like to send information about meetings, appointments, tasks, and paperwork, in addition to electronic messages? With WordPerfect Office 4.0 you can. It combines electronic messaging, group scheduling, and personal calendaring, integrating most of the functions work groups need in order to get work done.

WordPerfect Office lets you attach additional information or files—such as agendas, documents, presentations, or proposals for review—to your electronic messages. Users can assign tasks to co-workers. Notes can be scheduled to appear on a co-worker's calendar on specific dates, and WordPerfect Office's status-tracking capabilities insure that people who assign tasks know if and when a task has been completed.

Task Management

WordPerfect Office lets you schedule tasks for *other* people on your network, select the level of priority, and indicate the date the task needs to be completed. When a task is received, the person can accept, decline, or delegate it, and whatever the decision, the person who assigned the task will be immediately notified. When a task is accepted, it's automatically added to that person's task list with the priority level that was originally assigned.

Schedule Meetings

The frustration of trying to set up a group meeting is a thing of the past. With Scheduler you'll never again have to make ten or twenty calls in order to get four people in the same room at the same time. The process is easy. You select a list of attendees and decide the length of the meeting. Then Scheduler scans each individual's calendar for open dates and times and reports back to you the dates and times when *everybody* will be available. You then send out the meeting notice and let each individual accept or decline it.

Route Electronic Mail

WordPerfect Office's routing capabilities allow you to specify who gets your electronic message and in what order they get it. If you need three people to sign off on a business proposal, you can select the order in which the electronic message, and attached proposal, will be received. After the first person signs off, the message, with attachments, is automatically transmitted to the next person on the distribution list.

The Out Box

Whenever an electronic message is sent, the sender is notified as to what happened to the message. The Out Box tells you when each message was delivered, if it has been opened, deleted, or delegated. It will even tell you if a message has been deleted without first having been opened.

Other Features

In addition to electronic mail, group scheduling, and personal calendaring, WordPerfect Office 4.0 provides a calculator, a task list, a shared notepad, a shell menu, a notebook with an autodial feature, a file manager, a macro editor, and a text editor.

WordPerfect Office 4.0. WordPerfect Corporation, 1555 N. Technology Way, Orem, UT 84057; 800-451-5151. The suggested retail price for the administration and server package is $295, and the suggested retail price for a client pack with five mailbox licenses is $495. Licenses for additional users are available.

Put Your Name and Address Book and Your Computer in Your Pocket

If you would like to take not only your name and address book with you when you leave the office, but your computer as well, take a look at the Hewlett-Packard 100LX Palmtop computer. It's small enough to fit in your shirt pocket, coat pocket, or purse, and weighs only eleven ounces.

The HP 100LX palmtop computer is designed as a companion PC for people who need to travel light and want not only their computer files with them but their computer as well. All the software is built-in with read-only memory (ROM). Just push a button and you can go to your appointment book, to-do list, memo pad, Lotus 1-2-3, and the HP financial calculator from any other program within the 100LX. You can also send and receive electronic mail messages.

Personal Organizer

You've an appointment book and a calendar that shows a day-, week-, and a month-at-a-glance. The alarm feature will keep you on time for all of your meetings because you'll always have your 100LX with you.

And you can create your own to-do lists, as well as to-do lists for the projects and tasks you've delegated to others.

When you schedule an appointment or add a to-do item to your list, you can attach a note or memo to the item, so you can put your meeting's agenda with the meeting's appointment, as well as notes of any issues you want to discuss at the meeting. You can also use the memo pad to prepare your weekly status reports, take notes of your voice mail messages, and record your thoughts or ideas as you're walking down the street or waiting for an appointment. And when you go into your meetings you don't have to carry anything but your 100LX because almost everything you need, or want, is inside the palmtop, not back in the office.

Phone Book

When you travel with the HP 100LX you've always got your phone book with you—both your personal and business numbers. So when you need to call the pharmacy to renew a prescription, you've got the number no matter where you are. You can create separate phone books for your specific needs. Would you find it helpful to have a personal phone book, a corporate phone book, and a business phone book with the names and numbers of the businesspeople you talk to on a regular basis? If you travel, in each city that you visit you can keep numbers for car rental companies, hotels, and your friends.

Mobile Communications

The 100LX is designed for traveling professionals who need to communicate with their home office, customers, or clients using wired and wireless networks. You can attach either a serial or PCMCIA (credit card size) modem to a mobile telephone and you're ready to send and receive electronic messages, data, and faxes, no matter where you are. You can write text messages using the built-in editor, and include entire MS-DOS files with your message. You can download messages directly to your palmtop and read them instantly or store them for later.

Lotus's cc:Mail is built into the HP 100LX and can be used to exchange messages through an established cc:Mail post office with any cc:Mail user in the world. You can also subscribe to one of the messaging services that use advanced paging technology, which will deliver wireless E-mail messages, customized company data, news, stock reports, and more—while you're on the move. The mobile executive who can receive and send files and other information certainly has a competitive advantage.

Financial Calculator

The financial calculator is capable of performing general arithmetic functions, business percentages, time value of money calculations; interest rate, currency, and other unit (length, area, volume, etc.) conversions; cash flow reports, and statistical analysis. To solve specific problems you can create your own mathematical equations and plot the results on a graph. Once your calculations are complete, you can upload the data into a main database and have a report in a matter of seconds.

Lotus 1-2-3

The built-in Lotus 1-2-3 is an extremely useful application. You can develop fairly sophisticated macro-driven Lotus 1-2-3 models. You can create any spreadsheet and show it visually with the graph capability. You can rearrange your worksheet by copying, moving, and transposing data, or by inserting or deleting columns or rows. All of your worksheets can be saved to file, uploaded or downloaded to your desktop computer, and printed. You can automate your keyboard tasks with macros, and you can create your own formulas. And any collection of data that you organize in rows and columns can be used as a database.

The combination of small size and powerful applications makes the HP 100LX an indispensable daily tool for both your professional and personal life. It has enough memory to do meaningful spreadsheet calculations, good communications with a desktop computer, and a suite of applications that can do real work that are all loaded and can be opened simply by pressing a button.

It offers the familiar QWERTY keyboard, has an eighty-by-twenty-five-character liquid crystal display, and is powered by two AA batteries. The HP 100LX runs off-the-shelf DOS-based software with plug-in PCMCIA memory cards, and you can download software from your PC. You can print directly to your printer. And with the connectivity pack you can upload and download your phone book and every other file to your desktop computer.

You can even take it with you whenever you go shopping with your significant other. While he or she is trying on clothing, or doing something else that you find boring, you can occupy yourself by doing some work, or playing with your HP 100LX.

HP 100LX. Hewlett-Packard, P.O. Box 10723, Portland, OR 97219; 800-443-1254. Suggested retail price: $749.

Personal Information Managers for DOS

Though the majority of the new personal information managers that are being written today are for Windows, there are still some good programs that are available for DOS. Both Day Runner's Time Plus and WordPerfect's Office 3.1 are very powerful and easy to use. Either of them is a good choice if you haven't upgraded to Windows yet or if you're running DOS on your laptop.

Time Plus

Time Plus is an inexpensive, easy-to-use personal information organizer. It is well designed and well thought-out. If you aren't yet running Windows, it offers a very nice, easy-to-use program. The daily calendar and to-do list are designed to work together. The phone book will store all your names, addresses, and phone numbers and then dial the phone for you.

You can append a note to any entry in your calendar, to-do list, or phone book. If you have set up a Hot Key, F4, for instance, you can access your word processor to create and edit the notes as an alternative to using Time Plus's text editor. When you exit your word processor, you return to Time Plus.

One of the unique features of Time Plus is that it has a cross-reference feature. This allows you to see a complete chronological list of your current tasks, as well as a list of all the tasks or projects you have scheduled with any other people.

If you're already using a Day Runner personal organizer you can print any of the information that has been entered into Time Plus onto Day Runner pages that will fit into their Entrepreneur, Classic, or Running Mate personal organizers.

Time Plus. Day Runner, Inc., 2750 West Moore Avenue, Fullerton, CA 92633; 800-232-9786. Suggested retail price: $60.

WordPerfect Office 3.1

WordPerfect's Office 3.1 is available for stand-alone users. (Word-Perfect's Office 4.0 is available for networks only and was discussed on p. 47.) Office is made up of five modules that are all part of the WordPerfect Shell: Calendar, Notebook, Editor, File Manager, and Calculator. All of these modules are designed to work in conjunction with WordPerfect and use the same familiar WordPerfect commands. Even if you're not a WordPerfect user, you will still find WordPerfect Office to be a very powerful productivity-improvement tool.

Calendar

The Calendar program is an easy-to-use time organizer that lists your appointments, displays your to-do items, and provides you with a place to write daily memos.

The Print feature offers several options for printing Calendar information. You can print your calendar as a straight page format, or you can have your calendar printed in WordPerfect with WordPerfect's formatting capabilities and printers. When printing in WordPerfect, you can print to one of several Landscape or Portrait formats. These include an $8\frac{1}{2}$-by-11-inch Calendar format as well as different Organizer formats—$5\frac{1}{2}$ by $8\frac{1}{2}$ inches, $3\frac{1}{2}$ by $6\frac{1}{2}$ inches, 3 by 5 inches. This feature allows you to print your appointments and to-do lists on pages that will fit into your favorite personal organizer. You also have flexibility in selecting which items (memo, appointments, to-do) you want printed over different time periods (weekly, monthly, annually).

Notebook

Notebook lets you organize the information about your business contacts. Each notebook file is like a computerized box of three-by-five index cards. An accompanied index lists selected information from each card. You can create your own Notebook files, with separate fields for any kind of information you want. With a modem, you can use Notebook to dial phone numbers.

Editor

The Editor module is really two editors in one: a DOS text editor and a macro editor. You can use the text editor to edit programs and other files in DOS text format. You can use the macro editor to create and edit macros for Shell, Editor, WordPerfect, LetterPerfect, PlanPerfect, and WordPerfect Presentations.

File Manager

File Manager displays organized lists of directories and file names found on your hard drive or on a disk in a disk drive. File Manager's features help you find, organize, copy, and otherwise manage your files without your having to return to DOS.

Calculator

You can use Calculator to perform basic arithmetic calculations, as well as financial, scientific, statistical, and programming functions. Entries and results are recorded in a continuous *tape* display, similar to an adding machine. You can scroll through the tape, print it, or save it to a file.

WordPerfect Shell

Shell lets you organize programs and commands into a menu structure for easy access. Once you set up a program on the Shell menu, you just type a menu letter to start the program. While running a program from Shell you can switch to another program without exiting the current one. The Shell Clipboard offers a temporary buffer you can use to transfer information between programs that are running under Shell.

For the WordPerfect user, WordPerfect Office 3.1 offers a complete and total package that can help you improve your daily productivity by taking advantage of the many ways it interfaces with WordPerfect.

WordPerfect Office 3.1. WordPerfect Corporation, 1555 N. Technology Way, Orem, UT 84057; 800-451-5151. Suggested retail price: $149.

Computerized Name and Address Books

It's quite possible that you don't need a personal information manager, or you've become so attached to your personal organizer that you wouldn't even consider using anything else. But everybody has a need for a simple, easy-to-use telephone directory. Instead of keeping your list of important names, addresses, and phone numbers in your phone book or Rolodex file, store them inside your computer. If you still want to keep a paper-based phone book or Rolodex file, all you've got to do is print it out.

If you've got a lot of names and addresses to keep track of or other important information, here are some simple, easy-to-use programs. They'll save you hours of time, and you may find that you can actually live without the Rolodex file that's been sitting on the top of your desk for years. You'll even find that keeping these records can be fun.

Dynodex

Dynodex offers a simple, easy-to-use program for storing information on frequently contacted people or businesses. It is a superb address book that can provide you with a lot of flexibility. When setting up any phone book, easy data entry is one of the most important criteria. Dynodex makes it easy. There is a drop-down list box for almost every entry, where you can select from a list of previous entries. For example, if you're typing *Chicago*, you only have to enter it once. Whenever you need to enter *Chicago* in new records it will be entered automatically as you begin typing. This is a wonderfully useful feature.

Dynodex displays two windows: the Current Entry window, and the List window, which displays all the records in the current Dynodex file. The List Window allows you to quickly copy and paste a name and address from Dynodex right into a letter you're preparing with your word processor.

Dynodex's tutorial has several sample files that show off the program's power and versatility. There is a file with the names and addresses of the major restaurants in Los Angeles and San Francisco and a list of bed and breakfasts in San Francisco. Another file has all the numbers of the major airlines, car rental agencies, and hotels in

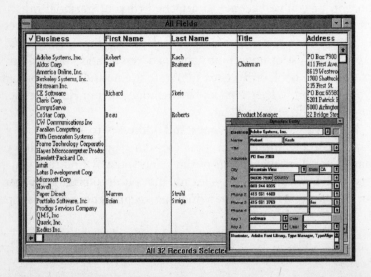

the United States. If your favorite hotel isn't on the list, you can easily add it.

They've also created a listing of every major software and computer company in the United States, with addresses, phone numbers, and a listing of their major products. In the notes section you can include your product ID number along with the companies' telephone routing codes. That way, when you call technical assistance, you won't have to listen to the long list of options and choices that come with a company's preprogrammed voicemail telephone answering programs. This should save you time.

One of the most powerful features of Dynodex is its ability to print address book layouts. Dynodex can print both single- and double-sided pages. If you like the idea of printing your name and address list for your personal organizer, this is a wonderful feature.

Dynodex is a complete program designed for managing names, numbers, addresses, and notes about the people and places that are important to you.

Portfolio Software makes two companion products that work together with Dynodex: Dynopage and Dynopaper.

Dynopage

Dynopage is a Windows printer driver that turns your laser printer into a virtual printing press. With Dynopage you can print almost any file to any layout imaginable. It gives you the power to print to any page size—single and double sided. You can scale the size of your printed page from full size to anywhere from 75 percent to 150 percent of the normal size. This is ideal for printing reports, documents, calendars, address books, lists, and trifold and fourfold brochures.

Dynapaper

Dynapaper was created for the person who wants to print the pages of their personal information manager and insert them into their personal organizer. Dynapaper uses perforated paper with prepunched binder holes that are designed solely to be used with personal organizers. The six-ring paper is perforated to yield three pages per sheet and works with Day-Timer Sr. Pocket, Day Runner Running Mate, or Filofax. And the half-page paper, which is perforated to yield two pages per sheet, fits into Day-Timer Jr., Day Runner Classic, or Franklin Day Planner organizers.

Dynodex. Portfolio Software, Inc., 10062 Miller Avenue, Cupertino, CA 95014; 800-729-3966. Suggested retail price: $89.95. The suggested retail price for **Dynapage** is $89.95.

Values Quest

Values Quest is a slimmed-down version of Ascend. It has only two modules: Values and Goals, and Address and Phone Book.

If you're interested in identifying what's important to you and determining where you want your life to go, you should consider purchasing a copy of Franklin Quest's Values Quest. It's an easy-to-use program that will help you answer the age-old question: "What do I want to do when I grow up?" Values Quest will help you identify your governing values—a belief or set of beliefs in which a person is willing to invest time, money, and energy.

Values Quest offers a comprehensive walk-through of the difficult process of determining your governing values and formulating

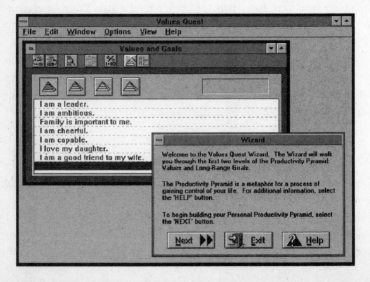

goals to orient your life around your values. This is done by the Values and Goals Wizard—an extensive database of examples of the values, goals, and clarifying statements that previous Franklin Day Planner users have shared with the company from their own experiences.

Setting goals is a four-step process. This process is designed to help a person align their daily actions with their values and goals. The Values Quest program will assist you in discovering the governing values that really motivate you. It will aid you in setting goals that will help you to do the things that you really care about.

Values Quest. Franklin Quest Company, 220 West Parkway Boulevard, Salt Lake City, UT 84119; 800-654-1775. Suggested retail price: $49.95.

Winfo

Winfo is a fun-to-use, well-thought-out Windows application for the small business owner and the person who uses a computer at home. Winfo comes with twelve predefined templates that allow you to track many of the different kinds of information that make up your personal and professional lives. These templates include a phone

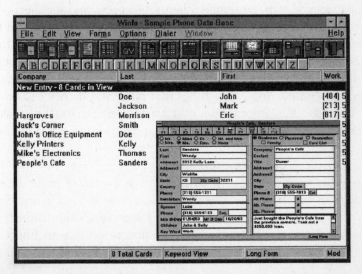

book, to-do list, sales contact sheet, mailing list, shopping list, home inventory, stock transactions, recipes, music/video/software collections, car and home maintenance records, and a format to keep track of favorite restaurants and hotels.

Winfo's directory is laid out in columns, like a spreadsheet. Its customizable views allow you to see your information on screen in any order that you would like.

Winfo. Win Ware Inc., 4665 Lower Roswell Road, Marietta, GA 30068; 800-336-5985. Suggested retail price: $49.95.

Improve Your Business Relationships with a Contact Manager

Contact management programs are information managers that are designed to help you keep in touch with many different people at the same time and to stay on top of everything that is going on between you and them. They have more powerful features than a personal information manager.

When you're working closely with many people—co-workers, colleagues and staff, customers, clients, prospects, and suppliers—you need to stay on top of everything that is going on between you and them. A contact manager provides you with the tools you need to do a more thorough job of keeping track of the information associated with your projects, tasks, and daily activities. This will allow you to spend more time doing the things that make you money because all of your important information is at your fingertips. You'll be making your deadlines and meeting your goals and objectives instead of making excuses.

Any piece of information about a person, project, or task that you would keep as a note in a file folder, as a scrap of paper on your desk, or as a mental note in your head, can now be kept in one place, inside your computer. You'll find that fewer things slip through the cracks because you have much more information at your fingertips, and you can put that information to good use.

In addition, a contact manager will help you to develop and strengthen your long-term relationships—which is the key to being successful in business—because they're designed to help you to get to know people on a more personal basis. You now have a place to store such information as the names of a person's spouse and children, the dates of their birthdays and anniversaries, and you can even note their favorite hobbies and outside interests.

Your Hands Never Touch the Keyboard

The beauty of these programs comes from the fact that they make it easy for you to enter information. Everything you would type as an entry appears in a pop-up box on the screen. You don't need to use the keyboard to schedule appointments, make telephone calls, or add to-do items. You no longer have to retype names, dates, or the purpose of the activity you're entering into your schedule. You just point and click with the mouse instead of typing away at the keyboard.

When you need to select an activity—schedule an appointment, add a to-do item, or write a reminder to make a telephone call—you select the name of the person from your telephone directory. Then you click on the activity you're scheduling, and a monthly calendar appears. Once you select the date, a daily calendar pops up so you can select the starting time and duration for the activity.

You use the mouse to select the purpose of the activity—send proposal, send quote, send follow-up letter, confirm meeting, close the sale, etc.—from a pop-up box that contains phrases or frequently used terms that describe the specific nature of your daily activities. (This pop-up box can be customized to display the specifics of your particular business or daily activities.) Next you select the priority level, and finally you turn on the alarm, so you will be reminded well in advance. You can also append notes of unlimited length. All of this has been done with the click of the mouse. Your hands never touched the keyboard.

To keep track of how you spend your time during the day, there's an automatic timer. This way you can keep a detailed record of everything you did and who you did it for, then print it as a report. This can be particularly beneficial if you bill for your time, or if you *really* want to see how you spend your time during a normal business day.

Keep Track of All Your Activities

Contact history records are useful for tracking your efforts and activities with a particular contact. Since each of your activities—meetings, to-do's, telephone calls, written correspondence, and faxes—with a person are done through your contact manager, you can see at a glance everything that has transpired or that you have scheduled. A record of each activity is automatically entered in the contact's history as the activity occurs.

Sending Letters and Faxes

Contact managers come with predesigned letter templates that make it easy for you to send letters, memos, and faxes. These templates can be easily modified. If you want, you can create your own letters.

Just select the contact and click on the letter icon. The entire letter will be created in an instant. This includes the date, name and address, salutation, closing, and text. You can then send the letter to your printer, or if it's a fax, send it to your Windows fax program. Letters can be created one at a time, or in groups, with the mail-merge features. Once the letter is written, a record of that letter is stored in the contact's history. With a DDE or OLE link you can view or edit the letter from within the contact's record.

Grouping Contacts Is a Valuable Productivity-Improvement Tool

Grouping contacts based on unique characteristics, or categories, is a valuable tool. Groups provide you with an easy way to keep in touch with many individuals at the same time. You can group your contacts in any way that makes sense to you, and you can place individual records in many different groups.

For example, you may need to view your contacts grouped by city, state, or area code; by occupation or profession; or just your "top ten customers." With the mail-merge features, you can select a group and then send the same letter to each member with just a couple of keystrokes or clicks of the mouse.

Creating Reports of Your Contact Information

One of the biggest timesaving features of contact managers is their ability to take the different pieces of information that you have about each of your contacts and use that information to create reports. You can generate reports of all your daily activities: meetings, telephone calls, and to-do's, including any appended notes, to see what you've done in the recent past and what you have scheduled in the future. This can be done on a global basis, showing you all your activities at once, or on an individual contact basis, where you can see the status of everything you have going on with one contact at a time. You can create your own format to show any information that would be helpful and meaningful to you.

These are six very good contact management programs:

ACT! Symantec Corporation, 10201 Torre Avenue, Cupertino, CA 95014; 800-441-7234. Suggested retail price: $399.

Desk Top Set. Okna Corporation, P. O. Box 522, Lyndhurst, NJ 07071; 800-765-5570. Suggested retail price: $195.

Commence. Jensen-Jones, Inc., Parkway 109 Office Center, 328 Newman Springs Road, Red Bank, NJ 07701; 800-289-1548. Suggested retail price: $395.

E-Z Track. E-Z Data, Inc., 533 S. Atlantic Boulevard, Monterey Park, CA 91754; 800-777-9188. Suggested retail price: $195.

Packrat 5.0. Polaris Software, 17150 Via Del Campo, Suite 307, San Diego, CA 62127; 800-722-5728. Suggested retail price: $395.

Sharkware, Harvey Mackay's System for Success. CogniTech Corporation, P. O. Box 500129, Atlanta, GA 31150; 800-947-5075. Suggested retail price: $129.95

Create Your Own Information Manager with a Database

A database offers you the ultimate flexibility in creating a personal information manager, contact manager, or information manager, because you can design precisely what you want and need from scratch. You can create your own to-do lists, call logs, project management status reports, holiday vacation schedules, and attendance schedules. You can use a database to keep an inventory of all the items in your office, for example, desks, chairs, computers, printers, or everything in your factory or warehouse. Once a database has been created, it can easily be modified and changed to suit your changing needs.

Viewing Information

The beauty of a database is that once you enter your basic information, you can then select different ways of looking at, or *viewing*, it. These different layouts determine the appearance of your information as you organize it for viewing on the screen—and then printing as a report. The information in your file exists independently of any layout, so you can design as many different layouts as you wish and arrange the information in any way you want.

Creating Reports and Form Letters

A report can contain information from many records, organized and summarized for communication with others. When you create a report, you can place the fields, graphics, headers, footers, and text where you want them to appear on the page. You can also have *calculated fields*. A calculated field lets you calculate values based on other information in the record. For example, if you're creating an invoice, one calculated field would show the total amount purchased, a second field would calculate the sales tax, and the final field would display the total amount due.

A form letter allows you to easily correspond with clients by using the database's mail-merge features. A word processor isn't needed. You create letter templates, which are then merged with one contact or a group of contacts and sent to your printer with just a few keystrokes or clicks of the mouse.

Automating Tasks with Macros

As previously noted, a macro is a single command that can help you speed up your work by automating regular or repeated tasks. For example, you might want to create a macro that searches for all invoices marked "unpaid," sort them by date in ascending order, switch to a past due notice report, and print the past due notices, all while you're on your lunch break. Or at the end of the day, you may want a report of every order that was placed, showing the largest order at the top of the first page and the smallest order at the bottom of the last page. With a group of macros, you can reduce your repetitive work to just a handful of keystrokes.

Database Uses Are Limited Only by Your Imagination

Any type of records that contain similar pieces of information can be stored in a database. You can create a database to keep track of sales leads or customer contacts. And if you want to store every bit of information about all of your employees, you can do that also. This could include the results of their employee reviews, and, with the object linking and embedding, you could include their picture.

A database can be used to keep track of all your business activities. This could include: Your invoices, inventory, daily, monthly, and annual accounting reports. You can use your database to send out bills and late-payment notices and create any type of form letter you want. Write a macro, and the whole process has been automated. All you have to do is decide what basic information you want recorded, and how you want to view it. The only limitation to the use of a database is your imagination.

These are three very easy-to-use database programs:

Ace File. Ace Software Corporation, 1740 Technology Drive Suite 680, San Jose, CA 95110, 800-345-3223. Suggested retail price: $199.

Approach. Approach Software Corporation, 311 Penobscot Drive, Redwood City, CA 94063; 800-277-7622. Suggested retail price: $299.

FileMaker Pro. Claris Corporation, 5201 Patrick Henry Drive, Box 58168, Santa Clara, CA 95952; 800-544-8554. Suggested retail price: $129.

Merge Your PIM, Contact Manager, and Database Files with Your Word Processor

Once you've set up your personal information manager, contact manager, or database, you may want a simple, easy-to-use utility program that converts your name and address records into your word processor's merge format. That's what MergeMaster does. It brings database files and word processing documents together quickly, easily, and seamlessly. Just select the database fields you need—name, address, salutation—and MergeMaster will create a word processing merge file that you can use to generate personalized letters, billing statements, and reports. MergeMaster works with dBase, Paradox, and the other major database formats and is compatible with all the popular word processors.

MergeMaster. Stairway Software, 913 First Colonial Road, Virginia Beach, VA 23454; 800-782-4792. Suggested retail price: $79.95.

Part II

WINNING THE FIGHT BETWEEN
YOU AND YOUR OFFICE

Use Your Computer to Send and Receive Faxes

One of the biggest timesaving and productivity-improving inventions in the last decade has been the fax machine. Over the past few years, the prices have dropped so low that almost everybody has one now. In fact, it's almost impossible to run a business without one. And though fax machines have made it possible to send and receive information in an instant, most of us still follow a cumbersome procedure. We print hard copies of that letter or document that we just created in the computer. Then we walk to the fax machine, insert the document into the paper feeder, and send the fax. This assumes that the machine isn't already in use. If it is, we wait.

And what happens when a fax is sent to you? Unless the machine is nearby, you have no way of knowing if a fax has been received. And what do you do if the fax machine is located in a different part of the office, or on a different floor? Do you get up from your desk at regular intervals to check and see if anything has come in? Whether it has been received, or not, you've interrupted your work flow, and if it has,

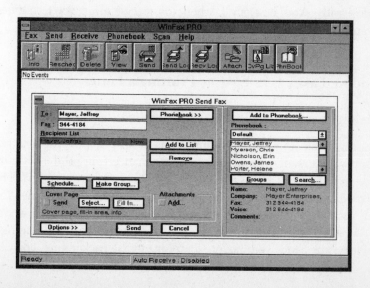

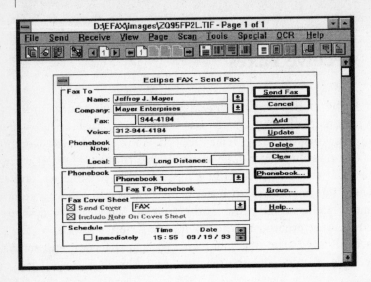

how long has the document been sitting there? Five minutes? Ten minutes? Or several hours?

Wouldn't it be nice if you could send and receive all your faxes directly from your computer? Now you can! And to make it even better, you no longer have to touch a piece of paper. There's no more walking back and forth to the fax machine, no more standing in line waiting for the machine to become available, and no more greasy, curly paper to deal with. And, best of all, when you receive a fax, you're notified instantly and can review it on screen or have it printed as a hard copy.

Sending Faxes Is as Easy as Printing a Letter

Sending Faxes from Within Your Applications

Sending a fax from within Windows is as easy as printing a letter. When you're ready to send your fax, you change your printer settings, select your fax software as the printer, and click the print button. The fax program is automatically launched, if it's not already running. You then look through your fax phone book, select the person to whom you wish to send the fax, add a cover page, press the SEND button, and it's done. Since your fax program runs in the background, you can continue using your other computer programs while the fax is being transmitted. Everything has been done from the keyboard in a fraction of the time it would normally take to send a fax from the fax machine.

Sending Faxes from Within Your Fax Program

You can also send faxes from within the fax program itself. Perhaps you would like to send a copy of the fax you just received to someone else, or maybe you just want to fax someone a quick note by writing the message on the cover page. The process is very simple.

You select the file you wish to fax, select the person to whom you wish to fax it, add a cover sheet, and once again press the send button. You can also group several different documents together—a letter from your word processor, tables from your spreadsheet, illustrations from your drawing package—so they can be sent in the same fax transmission.

Sending Scanned Documents

If you have a scanner, you can scan a document, newspaper article, photograph, or anything else and fax the scanned image directly from your computer. The scanned image can also be saved to disk.

Placing Your Signature on Your Faxes

Since you aren't handling a piece of paper, you aren't physically able to sign your letter or fax cover sheet, but you can import your signature on your letter. This can be done by either faxing or scanning a copy of your signature into your computer, where it is saved as a graphic image. When you want to sign a letter or fax cover sheet, you import a copy of the "image" and insert it in the appropriate place within your document. You can do the same thing with your corporate logo or letterhead.

The Phone Book

Another great timesaving feature of a fax program is the program's ability to create a phone book that contains the names and fax numbers of everybody you send faxes to. And if you want to send the same fax to several people, you don't have to send the faxes one by one. You can create groups of people in your phone book, and the fax program will send the fax to everybody in the group.

Let's say you wanted to notify your best customers or clients that you're about to release a new product. You create your announcement, select the group of people you want to send it to, click the SEND button, and all the faxes will be sent. What could be easier? To save yourself money, you can schedule a specific time of day when you want the faxes sent, such as after 5:00 P.M., when the phone rates go down.

Receiving Faxes

When you receive a fax into your computer, you've got a number of choices about how to handle it. You can have the fax immediately pop up on your monitor for instant viewing. You can be notified by a beep that you've received a fax and read it later, or you can have the fax sent directly to your printer, giving you a hard copy. No matter which option you select, you won't be interrupted or disturbed, because the fax is received in the background. Once you receive your fax, which has become a graphic image, you can do many things with it. You can read it on screen, print it, save it to file, or send it to someone else. Faxes can also be attached to electronic messages and distributed over the network.

Annotating Your Faxes

While you're reading your fax, you can write electronic notes to yourself in the margins or circle and highlight other parts of the fax that you think are important. When you've finished, the fax, with your notations, can once again be saved, printed, or sent to someone else.

Converting Your Faxes to Editable Text

One of the great features of fax software is its ability to convert a faxed or scanned image into ASCII (pronounced "asky") text.

ASCII is basic computer text that can be edited in any word processor or text editor. The process of converting a faxed or scanned image into text is called optical character recognition (OCR).

With OCR, you can eliminate the tedious and time-consuming job of retyping your faxes so you can use the information in another document. I'll be going into greater detail about OCR in just a little while. OCR technology takes a fax image (a series of light and dark areas on a page that have no inherent meaning to the computer) and converts it into text (codes that represent letters, numbers, and symbols that the computer recognizes). If you've got limited hard disk space, you may want to convert all of your fax images to ASCII text because ASCII takes far less disk space than a graphic image. These fax programs are very easy to use:

Winfax Pro. Delrina Technology Inc., 6830 Via Del Oro, San Jose, CA 95119; 800-268-6082. Suggested retail price: $129.

Eclipse FAX. Phoenix Technology, Ltd., 33 West Monroe Street, Chicago, IL 60603; 800-452-0120. Suggested retail price: $129.

Automatically Convert Your Faxes to Text

If you want to convert your fax's "images of text" into editable text, you don't have to perform the optical character recognition conversion manually. You can have your computer do it automatically whenever a fax is received. Calera's FAXGrabber is a fax conversion utility that controls and monitors all fax activity. When a fax is received, it automatically converts the incoming fax into a format that your favorite word processing program, spreadsheet, or desktop publishing application can read. Once received, the fax can be sent directly to the printer or can be viewed and edited. FAXGrabber makes it easy for you to incorporate some or all of the information from any fax into other correspondence.

FAXGrabber. Calera Recognition Systems, 475 Potero Avenue, Sunnyvale, CA 94085; 800-422-5372. Suggested retail price: $89.

Attach Your Faxes and Scanned Images to Your Documents

With Images you can *attach* your scanned or faxed images to any Windows word processing document, and then convert the image into ASCII text using optical character recognition. As you're reading your fax on your monitor, you can jot down your thoughts, comments, and ideas, using "sticky computer notes" and then save the fax image, with your annotations, to file.

Images. Image-X International, 5765 Thornwood Drive, Goleta, CA 93117; 805-946-3535. Suggested retail price for Images: $295. (Mention this book and you can get Images for $99.)

Turn Your HP LaserJet into an Automatic Fax Machine

If you're tired of greasy, curly fax paper, and have an HP LaserJet printer, you can turn your printer into an automatic fax machine with PrinterFax. PrinterFax is a cartridge that fits into the font cartridge slot of your HP LaserJet printer and allows you to take advantage of your printer's superb print quality. When you receive a fax, it's automatically printed as if it came straight from your computer's word processor.

PrinterFax. Moonlight Computer Products, 10211 Pacific Mesa Boulevard, San Diego, CA 92121; 619-625-0300. Suggested retail price: $259.

A Scanner Will Keep You from Drowning in Paper

The paperless office may still be a distant dream, but, with inexpensive, easy-to-use scanners, it is possible to keep your business from drowning in paper. Thanks to advances in scanning hardware and software technology, you can get excellent images from scanners—even hand-held models that cost just a few hundred dollars.

Handling paper is expensive, and filing is the one thing that everybody hates to do. Putting paper inside filing cabinets consumes a great deal of time and energy. That's why there's always a stack of papers sitting on the top of the filing cabinet waiting to be filed. Nobody wants to do it. And what happens when a letter or other document is needed? Someone must search through the file drawer and hope that the piece of paper is where it's supposed to be. If it's not, they must begin to search inside other files or rummage through those piles of paper that had yet to be filed and hope that it can be located in just a *few* minutes. Most people lose at least one hour of time every day looking for letters and other documents that aren't where they're supposed to be. In addition, a lot of expensive office space must be allocated for the storage of papers, files, and other records that are seldom if ever looked at again. With a scanner and OCR/indexing software, you can access any of your documents and records or view the information on your computer monitor in a matter of seconds.

An Index of Every Document's Key Words Makes Finding Any Document Easy

When a document goes through the OCR process, some programs also create an index, a list of all the key words in the document. When you want to locate a specific document, you type a key word or phrase, and the computer searches the index and displays a list of every document that has the word or phrase in it. This enables you to locate any document in seconds. If the list of files so revealed is extensive, you can do additional searches that will pinpoint the specific document you're looking for. Once a group of documents has been found, you can view the documents individually, to see which one has the information you need, or have them printed out. Scanning and indexing frees you from the chore of handling, moving, and shuffling paper.

What Can You Do with a Scanner?

What can you do with a scanner? Anything and everything. You can scan correspondence, newspaper clippings, magazine or trade journal articles, pages from a book, or any paper document, all of which will be available for instant future reference.

Both large and small organizations have been able to take their paper documents, files, and records and scan them into their computer, thus eliminating the need for extensive—and expensive—filing systems. These thousands of documents and records are now readily accessible to everybody in the organization. The scanned images of these documents can be accessed on their computer or through the network in a matter of seconds. The long wait for a file to come back from the file room, or a copy of a paid invoice from the accounting department, has been eliminated.

In addition to documents, you can scan pictures or photographs for use in your documents, computerized multimedia presentations, or for other internal corporate use. Once inside the computer, this image can be changed, manipulated, or edited in any way you like.

If you're creating a company telephone directory, you could scan photographs of each employee into the computer and insert the photograph next to their name, address, and phone number. In the personnel department, a photograph of every employee could be included in their corporate file along with other personal information that's contained in the database.

And, best of all, with optical character recognition software, you can convert a scanned image of a letter or document into the codes that the computer recognizes as letters, numbers, and symbols. If you spend a lot of time retyping printed information so that it can be incorporated into a document, letter, or report, scan it instead. You'll save yourself hours of time. You can scan newspaper or magazine articles, letters, reports, or any other printed information and immediately convert it to text that can be edited and formatted with your word processor.

For example, let's say you wanted to make some changes to a document that someone else had prepared. You can scan the document into your computer, convert the image through OCR into editable text, and make any changes you wish. If the document had originally been single spaced, you can change that to double spaced to make the editing easier. Then you make your changes, reformat it back to single spacing, and print it as a fresh, crisp, clean document.

Flatbed Scanners Can Eliminate Your Need for Filing Cabinets

You use a flatbed scanner the same way you use your office copier. Turn on the scanner, lift up the cover, and lay the piece of paper on the glass. The scanner is operated by your scanning software. Click the SCAN button with your mouse, and, within a few moments, your scanned image is displayed on your screen. Once on the screen, the image can be manipulated, enlarged, or shrunk. If it was scanned upside down, it can be rotated 90, 180, or 270 degrees. The scanned image can then be saved as is, converted to text through OCR, or indexed for future reference.

If you've got a lot of documents or other information to retain, scanning can be a very powerful way for you to store and keep track of them. You can attach a sheet feeder to your scanner that, depending upon the speed of the computer, scanner, and scanning software, can scan ten or more pages per minute. Scanning can also save you the expense of setting up and maintaining an extensive filing system to store information, and, as we all know, it's a very time-consuming process to file, store, and retrieve pieces of paper.

Handheld Scanners Are Great for Scanning Pictures

An inexpensive handheld scanner is an easy way to scan pictures and photographs for use in letters, documents, and presentations. The handheld scanner's sensors are in a small housing that is about four inches wide. To scan an image, place the picture against a light background and slowly move the scanner across the paper. If the picture or document is wider than the scanner, it takes two passes to complete the scan. Then special scanning software puts the image back together again once it's inside the computer. If you plan to scan photographs, a handheld scanner could be ideal for you.

How Does a Scanner Work?

During scanning, images are separated into thousands of tiny bit-mapped dots, also called pixels. The two most important variables in the scanning process are bits of data per pixels and resolution, which together affect how well (and how fast) an image displays or prints.

The number of bits of data per pixel determines the number of colors per image: one bit equals one color, 4 bits equals 16 colors, 8 bits equals 256 colors and 24 bits equals 16.7 million colors. The resolution, expressed in dots per inch (dpi), largely determines the image quality. Higher resolution means higher quality. The more dots per inch, the clearer the image and the greater the detail.

Both Envisions and Hewlett-Packard make a full line of black-and-white and color scanners. Envisions also makes black-and-white and color handheld scanners.

Envisions. Envisions Solutions Technology, Inc., 822 Mahler Road, Burlingame, CA 94010; 800-365-7226. Suggested retail price for black-and-white handheld scanners: $179. Suggested retail price for a color flatbed scanner: $899.

Hewlett-Packard. P. O. Box 10301, Palo Alto, CA 94304; 800-752-0900. Suggested retail price for a black-and-white flatbed scanner: $879.

Use Your Fax Machine as a Scanner

If you already have a fax machine you can turn it into a scanner. Image-X International has recently introduced ODIS (Office Document Imaging System). With ODIS, you attach your existing fax machine to your computer's fax card with a converter box. This allows you to send images from your fax machine directly to your computer without having to dial the phone. Once the document has been scanned, ODIS will index and store the document, which can be grouped within file folders, on your hard drive. It can then be retrieved in seconds by typing in key words or phrases.

ODIS. Image-X International, 5765 Thornwood Drive, Goleta, CA 93117; 805-946-3535. Suggested retail price for ODIS: $495. If you mention that you read about the product in this book, you can purchase ODIS for $295. If you need additional disk storage, floppy optical drives are available.

Scan Your Business Cards into Your Computer

How do you keep your business cards? Are they floating around in the lap drawer of your desk? Do you have a business card file? Or do you use a business card caddy—a vinyl wallet that holds four cards on a page? With a business card scanner, you can quickly turn those hundreds of cards you've collected over the years into a valuable database of easily retrievable information.

You simply insert the business card into the business card scanner and press the SCAN button. The computer software automatically captures the image, converts it into text, and enters the information into a name and address file. This information can be exported to many of the popular database and contact management programs.

CardGrabber. Pacific Crest Technologies, 4000 MacArthur Boulevard, Newport Beach, CA 92660; 714-261-6444. Suggested retail price: $395.

CypherScan. CypherTech, 250 Caribbean Drive, Sunnyvale, CA 94089; 408-734-8765. Suggested retail price: $395.

Convert Your Scanned Images into Editable Text with Optical Character Recognition

What Is Optical Character Recognition?

A scanner takes an electronic picture of a page, but you cannot edit a *picture* of letters and numbers. You need to convert the images in the picture into shapes that the computer *recognizes* as letters or numbers. The process is called optical character recognition (OCR).

Once these shapes have been found, the program then translates the patterns of the scanned image into textural characters and compares them with the characters it has in a built-in dictionary to see if they form actual words. After the image has been recognized, the programs have a verifier where doubtful characters—characters the computer has difficulty recognizing—are flagged for validation or correction. The document can then be edited and formatted like any other word processing document. The better the optical character recognition, the higher the accuracy of the conversion of the scanned image to text in the resulting document. The OCR program also recognizes the graphics that are on faxed or scanned documents.

Save Yourself Hours of Typing with WordScan Plus

WordScan Plus is an optical character recognition program that can save you hours of retyping time on every printed document you need to process. You can convert an entire page of text or selected areas.

As WordScan Plus processes your pages, it evaluates the letters and words and assigns a level of certainty based on whether the character closely matches the shape of a known character and whether the character forms part of a known word. When the program locates letters or words about which it is uncertain, the suspected image pops up. This gives you the opportunity to review the image yourself and determine the correct spelling of the word. The Pop-Up Verifier can save you an enormous amount of time proofreading because you don't have to refer to your original document to check recognition accuracy.

WordScan Plus also evaluates the layout of the page, saving important formatting information. The entire scanned document can then be translated into your favorite word processing format.

WordScan Plus. Calera Recognition Systems, 475 Potero Avenue, Sunnyvale, CA 94085; 800-422-5372. Suggested retail price: $295.

Store Your Documents on a Local Area Network and Get Rid of Your Filing Cabinets

Have you ever thought about how much space is being taken up by all of your paper files? How much time is used to file something away? How much time is used to retrieve it? What do you do when someone needs to access a file that's no longer in the filing cabinet or file room? Moving paper files and documents is a cumbersome process that is repeated continually throughout the day.

An alternative to file and paper management is the creation of an electronic filing system. You store all your documents and records on the network server of a local area network, and all of the users, known as clients, have access to the stored documents. With LaserFiche, you scan every document in your office or in the entire company into your computer, and the program indexes every word in every document. When someone needs to search for a document, they type in a name, word, or phrase, and a list of every document in the entire database that contains the word is instantly displayed.

LaserFiche is a computerized document archival system that allows access to documents by many users at once. Hundreds, or thousands, of documents can be entered into the computer every day. The OCR software fully indexes every word in every document and provides a system that can quickly and easily capture, organize, and retrieve most documents used by professional work groups. And since the user is working with images of the original document, there is no possibility that the original document will be lost or mishandled.

Any document within your computer can be indexed, including scanned images, word processing documents, and ASCII text files. In addition to the indexing, each image is given an index card that has a document name, and which can include additional information such as a description, action, type, date, author, subject, category, comments, etc.

Once a document has been retrieved, the text portion can be edited, and both the text portion and image portion can be printed. The resulting file can be saved, copied, or routed to someone else on the network, all without getting up from your desk.

LaserFiche. Compulink Management Center, Inc., 370 S. Crenshaw Boulevard, Torrance, CA 90503; 310-212-5465. Suggested retail price for the stand-alone version: $895. Suggested retail price for the network version depends upon the number of users. Five users: $4,995. Twenty users: $7,995. Fifty users: $18,995. One hundred users: $24,495.

Let Your Fingers Do the Walking . . . with a Modem

If you really want to expand your horizons, increase your knowledge, improve your productivity, and give yourself access to an almost unlimited amount of information, you need to attach a modem to your computer. A modem gives you the opportunity not only to communicate with other people using your computer, but also the capability to send and receive messages and files, access on-line information services, search thousands of databases, and share information through bulletin board services with people who have similar interests. But before I tell you about a few of the things you can do once you have a modem, I would like to explain how they work.

What Do Modems Do?

In order for two computers to communicate with each other, they must use the telephone system. In theory, that should be easy, in reality it's not. They each use different communications systems. The telephone system uses the analog form of communication, where the human voice is carried over the telephone lines, whereas the computer uses the digital form of communication, where the basic unit of data is the *byte*. (Each byte is made up of eight smaller units called *bits*. A bit is either a one or a zero.)

In order to send digital signals over an analog telephone system, a device is needed that converts the computer's digital signal into the telephone system's analog signal—both prior to and after transmission. The converter box that does this is called a modem, which is a contraction of the words *modulate* and *demodulate*. At one end of the call, a modem modulates the computer's data to produce an analog signal. At the other end, the receiving modem demodulates the analog signal, converting it once again into a stream of digital information.

When establishing a call, the modem operates much like your telephone. The modem dials the phone, and when the other modem answers, they begin "talking" to each other. (If the computer's speaker is turned on, you will hear a series of high-pitched whistles and other tones. This is how modems say "hello.") During their brief conversation, they are trying to agree on which protocols—data compression, flow control, and error control—to use. When they are in full agreement, the two computers are on-line and a stream of data begins to flow. If they can't agree on protocols, the modems hang up and the communication session ends before it ever began.

How Modems Work

The speed with which a modem is able to transmit data is measured in bits per second (bps). It is calculated by multiplying the *baud* (the number of times per second that the modulated analog signal changes state) times the number of bits (the smallest measurement of a computer's data that is transmitted). A 300-bps modem operates at 300 baud, transferring one bit of data per baud. A data transfer rate of 2,400 bits per second is achieved by sending 4 bits of data at 600 baud.

By adding a data compression feature, compressing the data before it is sent, modem manufacturers have been able to boost the performance of their modems significantly. For example, a 14,400-bps modem (the maximum speed at which data is carried over the phone lines) can actually achieve an effective data communication rate of 57,600-bps. This is done with a data compression feature, V42.bis, which compresses the data at a four-to-one ratio prior to transmission. When the data is received it is decompressed. Within the next year, a new class of modem will be coming on the market that will support data transmission rates of 28,800 bits per second.

Why Hayes?

Hayes Microcomputer Products has developed and sold more modems and communications software for personal computers than any other company in the world. Their most recognizable and widely implemented technologies have given rise to the description "Hayes compatible," which is prevalent in virtually any modem advertisement you see. These capabilities have led reviewers and analysts to use Hayes products as their benchmark for testing, a fact that under-

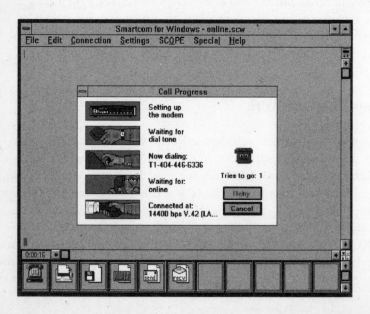

scores the recognition that Hayes products provide the features and technology against which other products are measured.

Hayes makes a number of different modems for various needs. There are internal modems, which are installed inside the computer, and external modems, which are connected to the computer with a cable. If you're using a laptop, notebook, or palmtop, there are both PCMCIA (credit card–size modems) and pocket modems. There are full-featured modems designed for users who need high-volume, high-speed data transfers; and there are modems designed specifically for use at home or in a small office.

Hayes Modems. Hayes Microcomputer Products, Inc. P. O. Box 105203, Atlanta, GA 30348. Call 404-840-9200 for a catalog, price list, and the name of your nearest Hayes dealer.

Make It Easy for Your Computer to Talk to Another Computer

Once you purchase a modem, you'll need software to help you use it. Hayes Smartcom communication software, available in five languages, makes the whole process very simple and easy. Smartcom helps you to connect to other computers and on-line services in order to retrieve information, transfer files, and perform electronic mail transmissions as well as virtually any other communication activity.

Smartcom makes it easy to create and start communications sessions. With its powerful scripting language, Scope, you can automate the typing of the information that must be entered in order to log on to and communicate with another computer. The full-feature text editor makes it easy and inexpensive to send messages. If you write your electronic mail messages before you log on to your electronic mail system, you reduce transmission costs. Smartcom has several different kinds of communications software packages available, depending on your needs.

Smartcom. Hayes Microcomputer Products, Inc. P. O. Box 105203, Atlanta, GA 30348. Call 404-840-9200 for a catalog, price list, and the name of your nearest Hayes dealer.

Modems Give You the Ability to Communicate with Other Computer Users

As I've previously mentioned, you can send and receive faxes from your computer. In addition, you can also send information between computers.

Let's say you want to send a letter, memo, document, presentation, spreadsheet, or even all the files in an entire computer directory to one of your colleagues or co-workers. You don't have to print the information and fax or mail it. Instead, you can send the whole package of information directly from your computer to his or her computer, using your modem.

Many newspaper reporters, for example, write their stories and articles on laptop computers. They then connect their modem to a telephone and dial their news bureau. Once connected, their stories are transmitted in just a matter of minutes. I also know of a number of authors who have collaborated on books while living thousands of miles apart. They use their modems to transmit files back and forth. And each day businesspeople all over the world are using their computers to keep in touch with their offices, customers, and clients.

Share Your Thoughts, Comments, and Opinions with Other Computer Users

With a modem you can log on to a bulletin board service. A bulletin board service (BBS) is a computerized message center and information service. Once connected, you can leave messages for other BBS users, read messages that have been left for you or the general public, download various files to your computer, and read information pertaining to the subject matter of the BBS. Today there are more than 50,000 bulletin board services, where you can use your computer to talk with others about almost any topic imaginable.

Get the Latest News, Weather, Sports, and a Whole Lot More

With on-line information services from such companies as America Online, CompuServe, Delphi, GEnie, and Prodigy, you can use your telephone to connect your computer to a broad array of information and interactive services. You can get up-to-the-minute news, weather, and sports, communicate with other computer users, and have access to thousands of databases. The following is a *very* brief summary of the services that are available.

Electronic Mail (E-mail)

Your personal computer becomes your personal communications center with your own private and confidential mailbox. You can send and receive messages from anywhere in the world twenty-four hours a day.

Electronic mail offers a quick and easy way to communicate with one person or several thousand people at the same time. You just type your message along with the person's name and address and press the SEND button. In addition to sending messages, you can attach computer documents to your electronic mail messages. For example, if you want to send someone a copy of the report you just created, you don't have to send it as a fax or print it on paper and mail it. All you have to do is attach a copy of the file to your electronic mail message and press the SEND button.

There are a few additional features of these electronic mail services that I would like to mention. You can send electronic messages to people who don't subscribe to an electronic mail service by sending either a fax or a letter. You create, and send, your message in the same way, but insert a fax number as the address instead of an electronic mail address. To send a letter, you insert the person's city, state, and zip code, and your electronic mail message will be delivered as a typed letter by the United States Postal Service or an overnight courier. To add a personal touch, the letter can be printed on your company letterhead and include your signature. (Of course, there is an additional fee for this service.)

Bulletin Boards

There are bulletin boards that cover almost every special interest imaginable. Here you can exchange information, seek advice, and ask questions. Messages can be posted on the bulletin board, where replies can be private or public. And there are open *conferences*, like a CB radio conversation, where everyone can "talk" at the same time.

News, Weather, and Sports

You can get up-to-the-minute coverage of national and international events, politics, sports, and the weather. You also have access to thousands of magazines and journals and can read the clippings from the national wire services as well as the stories that were written in the nation's major newspapers.

Business and Finance

Get the latest news from Wall Street and the world of business. You have access to a broad range of investment data, including information on stocks, bonds, options, commodities, and mutual funds. You can also buy and sell stocks from discount brokerage firms. And there are personal finance programs that can help you balance your checkbook, calculate your net worth, and determine the amortization schedule of your mortgage.

Research and Reference

You can have access to thousands of full-text databases covering every conceivable subject. There are even databases containing the names, addresses, and phone numbers of approximately eighty million people, so you can search for your old college roommate, the one you haven't heard from in twenty years.

Electronic Shopping

As an alternative to long lines and crowded parking lots, you can shop for many kinds of merchandise from the comfort of your own home and even get information on the costs of the newest model cars.

Personal Information

Make the most of your leisure time at home with extensive food and wine information, plus help with the car, the garden, pets, and practical advice on health and fitness.

Vacation Travel

Use your computer to make all your travel reservations from the comfort of your home or office. Take advantage of discount airline fares, hotel reservations, and car rentals.

The following are the major on-line information services. Each service offers a variety of different packages with different costs.

America Online. America Online, Inc., 8619 Westwood Center Drive, Vienna, VA 22182; 800-827-6364.

CompuServe. CompuServe Incorporated, 5000 Arlington Centre Boulevard, P. O. Box 20212, Columbus, OH 43220; 800-368-3343.

Delphi. Delphi Internet Services Inc., 1030 Massachusetts Avenue, Cambridge, MA 02138; 800-491-3393.

GEnie. GE Information Services, 401 N. Washington Street, Rockville, MD 20850; 800-638-9636.

Prodigy. Prodigy Services Company, 445 Hamilton Avenue, White Plains, NY 10601; 800-776-3449.

You Don't Have to Work for a Big Company to Use Electronic Mail

If you want to communicate with other people via electronic mail but don't feel that you need all of the additional services, you've got another option. You can subscribe to either AT&T EasyLink or MCI Mail.

AT&T EasyLink. AT&T EasyLink Services, 400 Interpace Parkway, Parsippany, NJ 07054; 800-435-7375.

MCI Mail. MCI International, 11330 19th Street NW, Washington, DC 20036; 800-444-6245.

Set up Your Own E-mail System

If you want to communicate with just a handful of people, you may not need to subscribe to an on-line electronic mail service that charges you for every message you send in addition to a monthly fee. With Personal-E Mailbox, you can set up your own electronic mail network and turn your personal computer into an automated electronic mail answering machine.

All you need to set up your Personal-E Mailbox system is two people who have the Personal-E Mailbox software. Once the software is installed, which takes only five minutes, your computer can call their computer, and you can leave electronic messages for each other. As long as the computer is on and the software is running in the background, you can receive messages at any time of day. There's no computer network, no complex hardware, and no network administrator. You don't even need a dedicated phone line because Personal-E Mailbox is designed to share the phone line with your answering machine and your fax machine.

To send a message, you write it in Personal-E Mailbox's text editor, select the person to whom you wish to send the message, and press the SEND button. Once the two computers are on-line, the transmission takes about thirty seconds. Long-distance charges are kept to a minimum because messages are composed and read off-line. Once received, a message can be printed and/or saved. A mailbox can also be created allowing you to leave messages for other users.

If you want to communicate with just a handful of people regularly, Personal-E Mailbox may be just the network for which you've been looking. At a price of $49 per copy, $79 for the twin pack, or $129 for the six-pack, this is a great little product.

Personal-E Mailbox. AmerCom Inc., P. O. Box 19868, Portland, OR 97280, 800-239-8295. Suggested retail price for a single user: $49; twin packs: $79; and six packs: $129.

Want to Get Attention? Send a Western Union Mailgram!

In business you don't make any money until a sale is made. And to make things happen often requires effective, timely, attention-getting communications. Today there are many different ways of communicating with people. You can write letters and memos, or send faxes and electronic mail, but if you really want to get someone's attention, send a Western Union Mailgram. And with Western Union's DeskMail, you can send a mailgram right from your computer that will be delivered with the next day's morning mail, anywhere in the United States.

You create your letter in either DeskMail's text editor or in your word processor. Then you use DeskMail's automatic dialer to log on to Western Union's computer. Once you're on-line, it takes just a few moments to transmit your letter. What could be an easier way to make a big impression?

If you want to send the same letter to several people, you can use DeskMail's merge feature to personalize each letter. DeskMail allows you to merge a list of names, addresses, salutations, and any other information you want to include into a form letter.

When I was trying to sell my proposal for this book, I sent a Mailgram as a follow-up letter to each of the editors who were reviewing my book proposal. I used the merge features to personalize the name, address, and salutation. Not only was everybody favorably impressed, I ended up with three offers and closed the deal within four weeks.

With DeskMail's Business Class service, you can have your company logo printed on the letterhead and a copy of your signature can be added to each of your letters. Business Class letters are delivered on the second day. (There is a setup fee for these features.)

With DeskMail, you can conveniently send your important business correspondence with the speed and impact that assures a quick and favorable response.

DeskMail. Western Union, Priority Services, One Lake Street, Upper Saddle River, NJ 07458; 800-336-3337.

Would You Like to Know the Weather in Tokyo, London, or Sioux City, Iowa?

Have you thought to yourself that your life would be easier if you knew how to pack for your business trips? Do you need light or heavy clothing? An umbrella and a trench coat or sunglasses and sunscreen? You can get the answers to those questions and lots more by using your computer to log on to the world's largest on-line weather service, Accu-Weather. This is the same weather service used by network TV stations, radio forecasters, and major US newspapers. With Accu-Weather Forecaster, you get instant up-to-the-minute weather information for anyplace in the world.

Accu-Weather makes more than two hundred full-color graphics available every day. There are displays of weather events, enhanced three-dimensional color satellite photographs, and composite radar images of the United States, Europe, and the rest of the world. There are contour maps that display the standard set of weather observa-

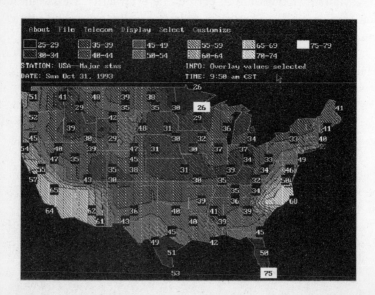

tions—temperature, wind speed, visibility, precipitation, etc.—that is reported every hour from thousands of weather reporting stations throughout the United States and the world.

When you want weather information there are two choices. You can log on to Accu-Weather's Accu-Data computer, browse through their database, and look at the high-resolution color images in real time. (If you call during a thunderstorm you can watch the lightning strikes on your computer screen even before you hear the thunder.) Or you can select the specific information you want before you dial into and log on to the Accu-Data computer. Once you're on-line, the Accu-Weather Forecaster's software will gather the specific information you've requested and download it into your computer, where you can view it at your own leisure. The process is so automated that the only thing you've got to do is tell the software to dial the phone, and that's done with the click of a mouse. The computer does the rest.

So if you're flying to London, Tokyo, or Sioux City, Iowa, you can get a detailed description of the weather conditions at this very moment and a forecast of the expected weather conditions over the next few days.

Accu-Weather Forecaster. The Software Toolworks, 60 Leveroni Court, Novato, CA 94949; 800-234-3088. Suggested retail price: $24.95.

Accu-Weather/Accu-Data. There is a subscription fee for subscribing to the Accu-Data database. For information contact an Accu-Weather Marketing representative at 814-234-9600, X400.

Run Your Computer at the Office from Your Laptop in Your Hotel Room

Have you ever felt frustrated because you needed access to a certain file that was stored in your computer at the office, but you were somewhere else? Or have you ever wanted to run a favorite program but couldn't, because you were working at home and your program was on your PC at work? If you answered yes to either of these questions, then you'll be very interested in a remote computing program.

In the past, computer users had to make a choice as to where their computer files and applications would be located—in their office computer, their notebook or palmtop, or in their computer at home. Now you can have complete access to all your information no matter where it's stored.

With a remote computing program you can run your computer in your office from your laptop in your hotel, or from your PC at home. And with remote computing you'll always have access to all of your files and applications no matter where you are—down the hall, across town, or a thousand miles away.

Through the use of a modem or over a network, you can control a *host* computer from any remote location and have as full access of the host as if you were sitting in front of it. Your keystrokes and mouse actions control the other computer, and your screen displays whatever is on the host's screen.

Anything you could do if you were sitting at the host computer can be done from the remote. You can run Windows and DOS programs, for example, retrieve, transfer, delete, copy, and print files. You can create and remove directories, check your E-mail, and use any device that's connected to the computer.

Using either the keyboard or the telephone, you can also *chat* with the operator of the host computer. When chatting with the keyboard the keystrokes of each person are displayed on both computers at the same time. If they wish to speak over the telephone, the remote computing sessions can be temporarily suspended. This comes in handy when there's only one telephone line for both voice and modem communications.

Carbon Copy. Microcom, Inc., 500 River Ridge Drive, Norwood, MA 02062; 800-822-8224. Suggested retail price: $199.

pcAnywhere. Symantec Corporation, 10201 Torre Avenue, Cupertino, CA 95014; 800-441-7234. Suggested retail price: $199.

Speed up the Process of Moving Files from One Computer to Another

How do you go about moving files from one computer to another? To move just a few files is no big deal. But what do you do when you need to transfer complete directories, software applications, or entire hard drives?

If you're trying to do this with floppy disks, it can become a rather difficult and time-consuming task. First, you must copy the data from one computer's hard drive onto a floppy disk that only holds 1.44MB (megabytes) of data. When the disk is full, you remove it, insert another, retype the copy commands, and wait for the disk to fill up again, repeating the process until all the desired files have been copied. To get the information into the other computer, you reverse the process. Fastlynx offers an alternative to all of this time-wasting activity. Just attach your computers with a cable and let Fastlynx transfer your files.

Fastlynx is a high-speed file transfer program that conveniently allows you to transfer files, directories, and complete disks of information among desktop, laptop, and palmtop computers. You connect the two computers with the special data transfer cables that come with the program. (If both computers are on a network, you can use the network to transfer the data instead of the cables.) Depending upon the configuration and speed of each computer, you can transfer data at rates of up to 8MB per minute. Once the computers are connected, you control both computers from a single keyboard.

To transfer files between the computers you use either your Windows file manager or Fastlynx's file manager as an interface or "menu" from which to copy, delete, view, and arrange your files. When the file manager is in the split screen mode, you can see the drives and directories of both computers at once. Transferring files is easy. You select the files you want to transfer, then the destination directory, and press the COPY key.

Fastlynx also allows you to access the drives, printers, and programs of one computer from the keyboard of the connected computer. This feature makes it possible for you to control your desktop computer by entering commands from the keyboard of your laptop or palmtop.

Fastlynx. Rupp Technologies, 3228 E. Indian School Road, Phoenix AZ 85018, 800-844-7775. Suggested retail price: $169.95.

Synchronize the Files on Your Different Computers

Do you have a computer at the office and a laptop or palmtop that you take on business trips? Do you work on computers located in different corporate offices? Do you have a computer at home? Do you keep copies of the same files on each of your computers?

If you answered yes to any of these questions, you have probably gone through this experience at least once: You made changes to a file, and, when you were done, you realized that you hadn't been working on the most recent version, because the most recent version had been created on a different computer. With FileRunner, you won't have any of these problems again.

FileRunner is a file synchronization program that makes it easy for you to transfer and update all your files on all the computers you use—anywhere in the world. This guarantees that wherever you go, you will always have the latest version of your files with you.

The program works this way: First you install a copy of FileRunner on all of your computers. Then you set up a transfer diskette, a floppy disk that has your mutually shared files. When you're finished working on a specific file you copy the updated file onto the transfer diskette and take it with you. When you're ready to work at a different computer you insert the transfer diskette into the new computer, and FileRunner automatically compares the date and time (Greenwich mean time, not local time—and daylight saving time is also taken into consideration) that the file was last saved with the date and time of the file on the transfer diskette.

If the copy of the file on the transfer diskette is newer than the version on the computer, it will then transfer the newer version to the hard drive and overwrite the older version. However, if FileRunner detects that the file in the computer has changed since the last time FileRunner made a transfer—a co-worker or colleague worked on the file while you were out of town—the older version will not be automatically overwritten. Instead, you're given the option of saving both versions. This way you won't inadvertently overwrite the changes that someone else may have made to the file.

When you're finished working, you copy the updated file onto the transfer diskette and take it with you once again. So no matter where in the world your different computers are located, as long as you have your updated transfer diskette, you'll always have the latest version of your files with you.

FileRunner has a virus detection program that will warn you if you're about to infect a healthy computer with a virus.

FileRunner. MBS Technologies, Inc., 4017 Washington Road, McMurray, PA 15317; 800-867-8700. Suggested retail price: $99.95.

Let Optionist Help You Make Better Decisions

For many of us, making decisions is very difficult. One of the reasons we find it so hard is because we're never 100 percent sure we've looked at all the available information from every conceivable angle. There's always the nagging thought in the back of our minds about some of the decisions we've made. These doubts exist because we feel that we may not have taken enough time to evaluate or examine other alternatives or choices before we made our decision.

During my business career, and throughout my life, I've had to make many decisions. There have been career decisions, investment decisions, personal decisions, and business decisions. Some decisions were good ones. There are others that I'd rather not talk about.

Years ago I learned a technique that has helped me whenever I need to make a decision: I put my thoughts on paper. Whenever I need to think, I pull out a pad of paper, ask myself some questions, and write down the answers. What am I trying to accomplish? What am I looking for? To analyze my options, I take a blank piece of paper, draw a line down the center. On the left side, I make a list of all the reasons why I should do something. On the right side, I make a list of all the reasons why I shouldn't. Then I think about the things I've written and try to make an informed decision.

Over the years I've found that when I've taken the time to write down, analyze, and think about the information I had available to me, I made a decision that I was comfortable with. (I'm reluctant to say the "right decision," or "the best decision," because in the end there may never be a right or best decision. I believe that as a person goes through life, it's important to look at the available information, think things through, and make a decision. The failure to do so often results in paralysis.) When I followed this process, I didn't second-guess myself very often. I did, however, think that if I could put this same information into a computer, maybe the process would be a little easier.

Now there is a computer program called Optionist that lets you harness the power of your computer to help you make better decisions. Its Seven Step Decision Method offers a framework that helps you organize, analyze, and evaluate all the information you have available, helps you think about what you're trying to accomplish, and assists you in making a decision. The Seven Steps are:

1. State your mission, set your goals, and identify what you're trying to accomplish.
2. Make a list of your options and alternatives.
3. Make a list of all the factors that will influence your decision.
4. Rate each of the factors that will influence your decision, and compare their relative importance.

   There are several ways in which you can compare the items on your list. You can rate each item on a level of importance from one to a hundred, or you could use Optionist's Pairs Comparison feature.

   The Pairs Comparison feature gives you the ability to compare each item on the list, one at a time, with every other item on the list. It then provides a summary showing which items were the most, or least, important to you. For example, if you wanted to determine which of five items on a list was most important, you would first make a list of the five items. Then you would put a checkmark by the item you felt was more important, comparing them each to one another, as shown below.

1 or 2, 1 or 3, 1 or 4, 1 or 5,
2 or 3, 2 or 4, 2 or 5,
3 or 4, 3 or 5,
4 or 5

The item that had the most checkmarks would be the most important.

This is a great way to determine priorities but is very tedious when done by hand. If you had a list of ten items to compare, there would be 55 total comparisons to make. If the list had twenty items, there would be 210 separate comparisons.

With Optionist, you type in your list of five, ten, twenty, or more items, and the program creates the comparison chart in a fraction of a second, no matter how long your list. Then you begin comparing one item to another. When you're finished, Optionist automatically ranks each item, showing you which was more or less important in relation to the others.

5. Evaluate your data. Optionist evaluates your list of choices based on the scores received for each of your decision factors. The Expert Advisor is available to analyze your data and make recommendations on how you can increase the accuracy of your decision model.
6. Verify and confirm that this choice meets your goals and objectives.
7. Act on your decision.

The final step in the Seven Step Decision Method is the most important of all. No matter how well-targeted and high-scoring your top option, it is of no significance unless it is implemented.

Optionist. Haven Tree Software, P. O. Box 470, Fineview, NY 13640; 800-267-0668. Suggested retail price: $299.

Help Your Direct Reports Become Better Employees

If one of your duties includes managing people, you'll love ManagePro. To manage people properly, you've got to help them set their goals and let them know what you expect from them. Then you must monitor their progress and offer feedback and coaching so they can do an even better job. And finally, once or twice a year, you've got to sit down with them to discuss their performance and review their salary.

To say the least, doing all of these things using just a pencil and a pad of paper is a time-consuming process, and for most of us, an organizational nightmare as well. It's difficult because we don't have an easy way to organize all of the information we accumulate, or should be accumulating, on each of our direct reports. ManagePro does it for you, and more.

ManagePro offers a complete set of tools to help you become a better manager. Its organized and systematic approach helps you stay on top of everything that you and your direct reports are doing and provides a framework so everybody knows what's expected of them. They know what they need to do, when it needs to be done, and what their reward will be when the job's finished.

With ManagePro you can plan, track, and organize all the information that you have about everyone's goals and action plans. And best of all, it's kept in one place. Here are some of the outstanding features of ManagePro.

Goal Planner

ManagePro lets you enter goals and objectives. You specify your group's goals and assign them to people or teams, or you can enter the names of the people or teams and assign goals to them. One glance at the Goal Planner shows you the status of everybody's goals and where you need to focus to keep them on track.

People Manager

When you sit down with each of your direct reports, you can help them set their personal and professional goals. Career development goals can be noted along with the commitments that are made to achieve those goals. Every bit of information that is entered into the People Manager is available for future discussion during performance and salary reviews. The results of the performance reviews can also be recorded, along with the praise that the person has earned for his or her outstanding work and performance.

Management Advisor

The Management Advisor offers detailed advice on how to improve management skills. Included are such topics as making better decisions, delegation of work, motivation, creating a sense of urgency, developing a feeling of ownership, and improving the use of time. These management tips and techniques can help you become a better manager and help your direct reports become more productive employees.

Instant Reports

More than thirty comprehensive reports are provided covering different views of each person's goals, people, or action items. Custom reports can also be created.

ManagePro. Avantos Performance Systems, Inc., 5900 Hollis Street, Emeryville, CA 94608; 800-282-6867. Suggested retail price: $395.

Take Complete Control over All of Your Projects

We've all got projects and tasks that need to be done. There are piles of paper stacked on the desk and around the office to prove it. But there are really two distinct classes of tasks or projects. There are the simple tasks, which can be completed in a few minutes, or hours. And then there are the bigger projects, the ones that will take several weeks, months, or longer to complete. These are the ones where big money is to be made. Their successful completion can have a big impact on the financial well-being of a company and a dramatic effect on a person's career.

I've found that when a person is organized, it's much easier to take control of a big project, since a big project is nothing more than a lot of little projects put together. Over the years, I've often suggested to my clients that when they have a project to tackle, big or small, they should start by pulling out a pad of paper and writing down every single task that needs to be done. When a project is broken down into very small increments, it becomes manageable, and the more detailed it becomes, the greater the likelihood that the work will be completed on time, done well, and remain under budget.

Once this list had been completed, the next step in the planning process is to write down the date that each task is to begin and when it is *expected* to be completed. Then look at each task individually to see how it relates to the other tasks. If work is to be delegated, this

FastTrack Schedule - [D:\FTSCHEDL\SIMPLE.FTS]

File Edit Schedule Command Alignment Font Style Help

Activity Name	Notes	Mar '93			
		7	14	21	28
New Product Packaging	Working with creative team. Final will be excellent.	3/8/93			
Finalize Design for Production	Check budget periodically.	3/8/93 — 3/14/93			
Artwork Production	Bluelines are critical.		3/14/93 — 3/19/93		
Approve Chromalins	Get copies for archives in addition to printer proofs.		3/19/93		
Packaging Production	4 color process needs additional laminate varnish.			3/20/93 —	4/4/93
Brochure Execution		3/12/93 —		3/30/93	
Approve Final Copy	Hank in charge of		3/15/93 — 3/22/93		
		7	14	21	28

should also be noted, including that person's anticipated time periods for completion.

Today everything that I had previously suggested a person do with a pencil and a piece of paper can be done at the computer with user-friendly project management software. The basic approach to organizing the work is the same, but the computer automates the entire process. You start once again by making a list, or outline, of everything that must be done. With the computer, it's easy to see the relationships that exist among activities. The more specific and detailed you are in itemizing and categorizing the tasks, the greater the likelihood that your project will be a fantastic success.

It's good to do this kind of detailed analysis with all of your projects or tasks. Completing the project is much easier when you have a grasp of all the details *before* you get started. By taking control from the very beginning, you minimize the chances of making serious mistakes.

Once you've listed all the activities that need to be done, you start analyzing how much time each activity will take and see if there are relationships among certain tasks. When will the task begin? When will it be completed? Which items can be done independently of the others? Which items must be completed before another one can begin? Which tasks have *float*, where a delay in the completion of that task will not affect the completion of the project? Which tasks are on the *critical path*, where any delay in their completion will cause an equivalent delay of the whole project? As jobs are defined and the relationship among them are established, you can calculate your schedule to determine the project's completion date.

For example, if you're building a house, the foundation must be laid before the walls and roof can be built. Or if you're creating a presentation, you may need to write it before you decide which illustrations, graphics, or pictures you want to include—and all of this must be done before it's sent to the printer.

Make a Picture of Your Project with a Gantt Chart

Once you've listed all the different tasks, including their anticipated starting and completion dates, these project management programs allow you to show this information visually in the form of a Gantt chart. The original Gantt chart, named after Henry L. Gantt, who developed them during World War I, was a hollow horizontal bar drawn against a time scale. The beginning of the bar identified the starting date of a particular task and the end of the bar showed the completion date. The length of the bar displayed the amount of time

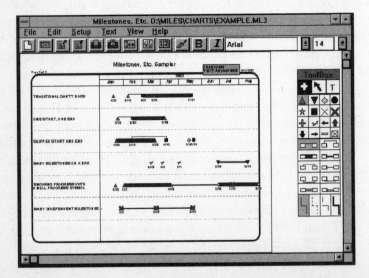

it would take to complete the task. As work progressed, the bar was filled in, showing the percentage of completion. A quick look at the calendar made it easy to see whether the particular task was ahead, behind, or on schedule. Gantt charts are a proven productive way to plan and schedule any project.

In creating your computerized Gantt chart, you itemize all your tasks and define the period of time by which you wish to measure progress: hourly, daily, weekly, monthly, quarterly, or annually. Then you use the mouse to drop and drag the starting and completion dates of the horizontal bar on the chart. The length of the bar shows how long the task is expected to take. You can use different types of shading for each line, and different shapes or symbols can be used to represent the starting and completion dates. On your chart you can show *milestones*, key or important checkpoints in a project, along with detailed notes and descriptions of each task.

Once you've drawn your Gantt chart, you can show the interdependency among tasks and indicate that one task must be completed before another task can begin. Referring back to my earlier example, you can show on your chart the relationship that exists between the foundation of the house and the walls. If there is a delay in laying the foundation, there will be an equivalent delay in the commencement of the construction of the walls.

One of the nice features of these project management programs is their ability to print out complete schedules and charts and export the information for use with a spreadsheet or word processing program. This allows you to use this information whenever you need to prepare progress or status reports for the other members of your team, upper levels of management, or your customer.

Milestones, Etc. Kidasa Software, 1114 Lost Creek Boulevard, Austin, TX 78746; 800-765-0167. Suggested retail price: $189.

Gantt Chart. Prisma Software Corporation, 2301 Clay Street, Cedar Falls, IA 50613; 800-437-2685. Suggested retail price: $89.

Project Scheduler. Scitor Corporation, 393 Vintage Park Drive, Foster City, CA 94404; 415-570-7700. Suggested retail price: $695.

FastTrack Schedule. AEC Software, 22611 Markey Court, Sterling, VA 20166; 800-346-9413. Suggested retail price: $279.

Explain Your Tasks with Pictures Instead of Words

Have you ever tried to explain a task to someone and, after a few minutes, realized that he or she didn't fully understand it? So out of frustration you pulled out a pad of paper and drew several boxes. In each box you wrote a brief description of the specific task, numbered the boxes 1, 2, and 3, and for further clarity, connected them with arrows. You may not have known it, but you drew a flowchart.

Flowcharts have long been recognized as one of the most important, and easiest, ways to communicate ideas effectively between people. The concept behind a flowchart is simple: A symbol is used in place of a long written explanation. Each symbol in a flowchart— a diamond, rectangle, circle, or square—represents something. The boxes are connected with arrows so the person can see the flow, progression, or relationship from one step to the next.

What can you do with a flowchart? Any set of instructions can be turned into a flowchart. And, by taking the time to identify each step in the process, you can look for the bottlenecks that cause the flow of work to slow down. Once those bottlenecks are identified, the process can be modified or changed. The end result is a smoother running operation, with better efficiency.

Here are just a few of the ways flowcharts help improve productivity and improve the flow of communication between people:

- They help an office manager describe a filing system to a clerk or the operation of the telephone system to a temporary employee.
- They let a chemical engineer teach a complicated testing process to a lab technician.
- They make it possible for a businessman to explain his company structure to the bank officer who is reviewing his loan application.

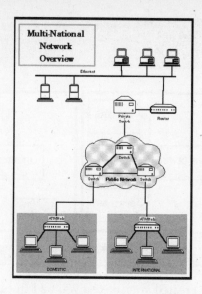

- They allow a department head to prove the need for additional employees.
- In a manufacturing company, a flowchart can show the steps that need to be followed to enter an order into the system.
- Attorneys use flowcharts to diagram estate plans and show the relationships among parties.

The list goes on and on. In fact, almost any process can be reduced to some boxes with lines connecting them. Why don't more people use flowcharts? Because they aren't easy to create. That is, until now!

Computerized Flowcharting Makes Drawing Symbols, Lines, and Text Easy

With computerized flowcharting software, you can now create a flowchart in a matter of minutes. You click on a shape with the mouse, position the cursor on the desktop, click the mouse again, and a box appears. Move the cursor to another location, click the mouse, and a second box appears. To change the position of a box, you drag and drop the box to another location.

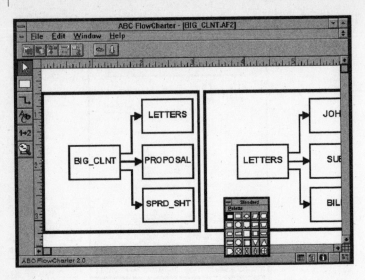

Once you've created your boxes, you add lines by changing the cursor to "line draw." Position the cursor where you want the line to start, hold down the left mouse button, and drag the cursor to where you want the line to end. Release the button, and the line appears.

Shapes can be made smaller or larger by clicking on a corner of the box and dragging it inside or outside. Once your flowchart layout is complete, you can then place text inside the boxes and alongside the lines.

All of these programs come with several different shape libraries and have shape editors that give you the ability to modify existing shapes or create your own.

Flow Charting 3. Patton & Patton Software Corporation, 485 Cochrane Circle, Morgan Hill, CA 95037; 408-778-6557. Suggested retail price: $250.

EasyFlow. HavenTree Software Limited, P. O. Box 470, Fineview, NY 13640; 800-267-0668. Suggested retail price: $280.

ABC FlowCharter for Windows. Micrografx, 1303 Arapaho Road, Richardson, TX 75081; 214-234-1769. Suggested retail price: $495.

FlowChart for Windows. Prisma Software, 401 Main Street, Cedar Falls, IA 50613; 800-437-3685. Suggested retail price: $89.

Let Your Mouse Create Your Organizational Charts

If you've ever spent time trying to design a company or departmental organizational chart with a plastic template and a ruler, you know that it's a tedious and time-consuming progress. For that reason, though organizational charts can be very helpful, they are very seldom created and are updated even less frequently.

With Micrografx's Windows OrgChart, creating boxes is easy. You can now create, edit, and print high-quality organizational charts and tree diagrams in minutes instead of hours. It's as simple as pointing at boxes and clicking with the mouse.

There is a master icon that is made up of several icons, each representing a type of position: A manager, co-worker, assistant, and subordinate. To add a box, or group of boxes, you select the type of

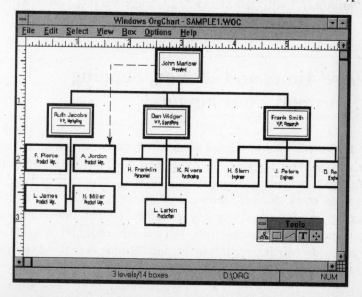

box you want by positioning the cursor on the appropriate icon and clicking. If you want to add three assistants, you hold down the shift key and click the mouse three times. The lines connecting the boxes are drawn automatically.

To add additional boxes, you simply move the cursor to the desired position, select the type of box you want to add, and start clicking. As you add more levels to a chart, the chart expands horizontally. With the click of the mouse, you can change the layout of the horizontal and vertical columns; the size, position, and color of the boxes; and the configuration, color, and thickness of the lines connecting them.

Once you've created your chart, you can include as much or as little information about the person or position as you like. In addition to name and title, you can add additional fields of information such as salary, date of hire, or last raise. You have the option of displaying every field of information or keeping certain fields confidential, and you can display pictures of everyone in your chart.

Keeping your chart up-to-date is easy. Whenever there are personnel changes, just make your changes and the chart is instantly updated.

Windows OrgChart. Micrografx, Inc., 1303 Arapaho Road, Richardson, TX 75081; 800-733-3729. Suggested retail price: $149.

Are Time, and Money, Slipping Through Your Fingers?

Have you ever wondered where the time went during an eight-, ten- or twelve-hour day? You can now find out with Timeslips. Timeslips is an outstanding time management tool designed to help you keep track of every moment of your day—your phone calls, meetings, the time spent writing letters and memos, drafting reports, and working on specific projects—so you can record all of your time, itemize what you did, record the amount of time it took you to do it, and bill it appropriately. Timeslips will also keep track of any expenses you incur as part of your work for the client—photocopies, postage, mileage, faxes, and charges for overnight deliveries. Once you've recorded your time and associated expenses, Timeslips prepares an invoice.

Timeslips has an impressive list of worksheets, reports, graphs, and user-defined reporting options that let you analyze your time and expense data in dozens of illuminating incisive formats. It's a sophisticated database manager that automates crucial professional tasks: tracking time and expenses, printing custom invoices, recording client transactions, managing multiple projects—while maintaining a clear audit trail.

Timeslips can also help keep track of the real costs incurred when a task or project is being billed at a flat rate or fee. This lets you know if you're overutilizing or underutilizing your time and resources. If, for instance, you bid a project, anticipating that it would take you fifteen hours to complete, did you actually complete the work within fifteen hours? If not, why not? Did you underestimate the complexity of the job, or did the job take longer than expected because of inefficiencies? With Timeslips, you'll know the answer and thus the solution.

If you need to accurately account for your time or manage people who are paid by the hour, Timeslips is for you. It makes time and billing more complete and thorough and captures billable hours that otherwise might be lost. And even if you're not billing a client for all of your time, you can show the time that was expended but was not billed on the invoice.

Timeslips. Timeslips Corporation, 239 Western Avenue, Essex, MA 01929; 800-285-0999. Suggested retail price: $299.95.

Do You Know How Your Staff Members Are Spending Their Time?

There's an old saying that "time is money," and even if you don't bill by the hour, being unable to keep track of how much time

	TimeSheet Professional								
Files Edit Timesheet Summary Detail								Help	
Mitch Russo				1991					
10/24/91	$0.00	Thu	Fri	Sat	Sun	Mon	Tue		
AZI	PubOff	2Res				6.0			6.0
AZI	PubOff	Feasibl	5.0	2.0	1.75				8.75
AZI	PubOff	Plan		1.0	6.25	2.0			9.25
ConRail M&S	Course			5.0					5.0
ConRail M&S	FocusG								
ConRail M&S	Plan								
ConRail M&S	Train	3.0							3.0
Oper	Holiday								
Oper	Off-sit								
Oper	Vacatio								
PacFax M&S	Course								
PacFax Needs	Course								
PacFax Needs	Train								
NOTE EXPENSE +TIME Timer		8.0	8.0	8.0	8.0				32.0
Arizona Instruments - Public Offering - Secondary Research									

you, or your staff, spent on a particular task or project can be very expensive.

We all know that every hour counts when you're working on projects or with clients. But tracking time and expenses can be as time consuming as the work itself—and a lot more tedious. Time$heet Professional takes the burden out of tracking time and expenses.

Time$heet Professional is designed to help you keep track of how time is spent during a day so that time can be properly allocated between clients and projects. This information can then be used for billing purposes and can help you determine if a project is taking longer than it should, or if it's right on schedule.

The program looks like a basic spreadsheet. Days are displayed across the top, and the task list—including client, project, activity, and any other descriptions you care to add—is down the side. Each cell in the central portion of the window represents the amount of time devoted to a specific task on a particular day. Like a spreadsheet, the far-right column shows the billing by client for the week. At the bottom of the page, the total billing for the day is displayed. The cumulative weekly billing is displayed in the bottom right-hand corner.

Time$heet Professional is designed to help you manage the time allocated to a project so you can see how long each part of the project has taken and whether it has exceeded or is under the estimated time when the work was bid. Having time data instantly available to project managers and the accounting department means that project management reporting is more accurate and schedules are kept on track. Time$heet Professional is designed to work with many of the top project management programs. The task list can be imported from your project management program into Time$heet Professional. Then the actual hours and associated costs are exported back into the project management program.

Notes and expenses can be added to each item. These notes are a useful way to maintain a project diary. They can be included in reports and on invoices, adding detail to work items. And by associating expenses with a client as they occur, it becomes much easier to keep a detailed record of costs you are incurring on behalf of the client.

Every item recorded on a time sheet—hours, notes, and expenses—can be collected, organized, and printed with a custom Detail Report. The Detail Report can serve as a client invoice, as a project log, or as an expense report.

When a job is performed on a fixed-fee basis, the program lets you track your time on the project while still charging a standard fee. This allows you to track hours against the project without a time charge appearing on the Detail Report when invoices are prepared.

With the stand-alone or network version, you can enter times to each of your projects throughout the day as they occur. If you're the office administrator and have the only copy of Time$heet Professional, you can print out a template for every employee with a listing of all their clients, projects, and tasks. The billable time is filled in by hand and, at the end of the week, is turned in as their time sheet. When the sheet's returned, it will take you just a few minutes to enter the information into the computer.

Time$heet Professional. Timeslips Corporation, 239 Western Avenue, Essex, MA 01929; 800-285-0999. Suggested retail price: $199.95.

Complete Your Expense Reports in Just a Few Minutes

Does this sound familiar? You've just returned from a business trip. On your desk is a huge stack of mail, next to the phone is a pile of messages, and your calendar is booked solid with people who need to meet with you. If you were to look at your to-do list at this very moment, the last item would probably be "fill out expense report."

Filling out expense reports is a very tedious and time-consuming task. Your receipts must first be sorted by day and by expense category. Then the information must be entered onto the form by hand, and the columns must be added vertically and horizontally. When you're finished, you can only hope the arithmetic matches in the bottom right-hand corner.

And when you *think* you're finished, you always find one last receipt that was buried in a drawer, or stuffed inside a coat pocket. You stop for a moment, look at the receipt, and ask yourself: "Do I want to take the time to recalculate the entire report? Is it *really* worth it?" If the amount of the receipt is small you probably decide to skip it. But those miscellaneous receipts can add up to hundreds or thousands of dollars of unreimbursed expenses over a year. To say the least, completing expense reports is one of the most unproductive tasks we're required to do.

Expense It! is an easy-to-use program that simplifies the whole process of completing expense reports. In just a matter of minutes you can enter all your expense items, print a report that is itemized by both city and date, and send it on its way. Once you enter your receipts, the items are sorted by date and category and a report is generated, with all the arithmetic in order. And should you find a receipt that you forgot, simply enter it and print an updated report.

If your expenses were incurred in a foreign currency, a Currency Calculator will convert those expenses into US dollars. Expense It! also takes into consideration the IRS's current year allowance for meals and entertainment expenses. You can also specify the type of auto allowance or deduction you're entitled to.

If you must fill out your expense report on a company form, Expense It! has a custom layout feature that allows you to position your Expense It! information so each expense item will appear in the appropriate box on your company's form. For a fee, On The Go Software will create the expense report template for you.

Expense It! On The Go Software, 4225 Executive Square, LaJolla, CA 92037; 619-558-4114. Suggested retail price: $129.99.

Put an End to Paper Forms and Throw away Those Interdepartmental Envelopes

Would you like to put an end to office paperwork? Well, I'm sorry, you can't! But with WordPerfect InForms and some help from your electronic mail system, you won't have to touch another piece of paper again. With InForms, you use the computer to design a form that is stored as an *electronic* template. It can then be completed from within the computer and sent over the network as electronic mail, guaranteeing instant delivery, or printed and sent through traditional distribution channels.

You can use InForms to create any type of form. In fact any form, paper or electronic, that your company uses can be created in-house. For instance, you can create expense reports, surveys, questionnaires, applications, equipment requisitions, loan request forms, bills of lading, and purchase orders. A form can be up to ninety-nine pages in length.

Electronic forms are dynamic and interactive. They can execute sophisticated mathematical and statistical calculations, retrieve information from databases, check for misspelled or misplaced entries, and protect confidential information. They can even display instructions, should the person completing the form have any questions. And finally, each response can be saved directly to a database.

You build forms by selecting objects from the Informs Designer tool palette and, with a quick click and drag of the mouse, place them on-screen. To give your form a distinctive look, you can add graphic images, insert colored boxes, circles, and lines, and choose fonts with different styles, sizes, and colors. To make your form functional, there are entry fields, radio buttons, action buttons, check boxes, tables, bar codes, and drop-down list boxes. InForms comes with a hundred ready-made forms that you can easily modify to suit your specific needs. Any form that you create can be printed and used as a *traditional* paper form.

Should a form require an authorized signature, WordPerfect InForms includes an electronic signature security feature. Once a form is signed a "tamper seal" is attached to protect the form from unauthorized changes.

WordPerfect InForms. WordPerfect Corporation, 1555 N. Technology Way, Orem, UT 84057; 800-451-5151. The cost of InForms depends upon the number of users on your network. The suggested retail price for the stand-alone version is $495.

Communicate Your Ideas with Pictures

No matter what kind of work you do, chances are that you use graphics to communicate your ideas. With Visio, you can produce a wide range of professional-looking business and technical drawings in minutes, and you don't have to be a graphic artist or draftsman to do it.

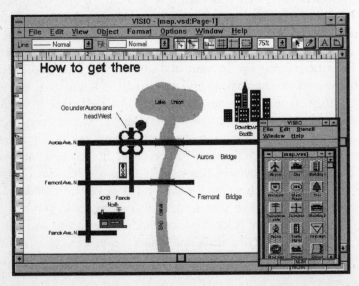

Visio's templates come with ready-made easy-to-use shapes. There are basic shapes: squares, triangles, arrows, and other useful master objects. There are also shapes for creating block diagrams, flowcharts, Gantt charts, and shapes used in space and office planning. There are shapes containing outline maps of the states in the United States of America, the countries in Europe, and the major continents and regions of the world. You can even create your own directional maps. And there are shapes that can be used to create awards certificates, office forms, fax cover sheets, letterheads, and business cards.

By just clicking your mouse, Visio lets you drag and drop shapes, change their size and color, connect them automatically, and type in text for labels, legends, or titles. With its straightforward stencils, simplified tool set, and common sense approach to drawing, Visio makes drawing easy.

Visio. Shapeware Corporation, 1601 Fifth Avenue, Seattle, WA 98101; 800-446-3335. Suggested retail price: $299.

Use CorelDRAW to Design Your Advertisements, Brochures, Flyers, and Mailing Pieces

If you need a drawing program for your corporate advertisements, brochures, flyers, mailing pieces, or multimedia presentations, you should take a look at CorelDRAW. It is made up of seven separate modules that make it easy for you to create graphics, charts, slide shows, animations, and a whole lot more.

The program is huge. It comes on twelve floppy disks and two CD-ROMs. To install the entire program you'll need about 40 megabytes of hard disk space. However, with the CD-ROMs you have another option. You can run the program from the CD-ROMs themselves, and when you do that you only need about 4 megabytes of disk space.

CorelDRAW comes packed with tools that will make your graphics, illustrations, and presentations stand out from the crowd. There are 750 fonts in both TrueType and Adobe Type 1 formats that can be used in CorelDRAW or any other Windows application. And there are more than 18,000 pieces of editable clip art (the CD-ROMs hold more than 1,000 megabytes of graphic, animation, and sound files). These are grouped together for easy viewing in the visual file manager, CorelMOSAIC, and can also be studied in the inch-thick book that comes with the program. This book displays each of the font typefaces and has "thumbnail" illustrations of each of the clip art images. The following is a brief summary of each of the CorelDRAW modules:

CorelDRAW

CorelDRAW is an ideal tool for virtually any design project—from logos and product packaging to technical illustrations and advertisements. When you create graphics with CorelDRAW, you begin by drawing simple objects: rectangles, ellipses, straight and curved lines and text. Once an object has been drawn, you can transform, or change, its orientation or appearance—Stretch, Scale, Rotate, Skew, and Mirror—without altering its basic shape.

Then you can manipulate your objects: The Envelope feature lets you distort objects. The Blend feature blends the shape and color of one object with that of another. The Extrude feature projects surfaces from an object to give it a three-dimensional appearance. And, the Contour command produces a series of concentric shapes that give an object the illusion of depth. The width, shape, and color of each object's outline can be varied with the Outline Pen. You can also adjust the pen's nib shape, a powerful feature that allows you to mimic the style characteristics of a calligraphic pen.

With the Fill Tool you can fill the interiors of objects with different shades of gray, color, and full-color patterns. CorelDRAW comes with a number of different color pallets—there are more than 700 spot colors to choose from—and there is a vast assortment of fountain (gradient) fills, patterns, and textures.

The Windows Clipboard can be used to import text from other CorelDRAW files, other applications, and text that was created in more than twenty different word processors. The Symbols Library has a collection of over 5,000 professionally drawn symbols covering such diverse topics as business, the environment, science, and transportation. Each symbol can be edited just like any other CorelDRAW object. And the Bullet Library has more than 5,000 bullet styles to choose from.

CorelPHOTO-PAINT

CorelPHOTO-PAINT is an image editor that gives you the power to produce paintings and photo-realistic images for all your presentations, brochures, and documents. It has an impressive list of painting tools and numerous image-enhancing special effects filters that can improve the appearance of both your images and scanned pictures.

The painting tools consist of a series of paint brushes that are used to create on-screen brush strokes. There are also some *special* paint brushes. The Impressionist Brush paints with multicolored brush strokes, the Pointillist Brush creates clusters of dots, and the Artist Brush gives your image the appearance of an oil painting. You can also draw lines, curves, ellipses, polygons, and rectangles.

The retouching tools give you the ability to fine-tune selected areas of an image, and with the filters you can enhance an image's appearance and create special effects for part or all of an image. With them you can erase areas of a picture, replace color, adjust contrast, control brightness, tint an image; and blend, smudge, sharpen, and smear specific areas of an image. There are more than thirty different types of filters that can be used to enhance your picture or image. On the CD-ROM there are hundreds of images that can be used with CorelPHOTO-PAINT.

CorelTRACE

CorelTRACE converts bit-mapped images—the kind that paint programs like CorelPHOTO-PAINT and scanners create—to vector images and editable text. When you convert bit maps, such as scanned pictures, to vector artwork you give your artwork smooth lines because you have removed the jagged edges of the bit-mapped image.

CorelCHART

With CorelCHART you can build all types of charts and graphs—from line, bar, and pie graphics to three-dimensional, area, and pictographs—that will help you easily express your ideas and information. On the CD-ROM there are hundreds of CorelCHART templates to choose from. You can enter chart data directly into the program's Data Manager, or you can import data from many of the popular spreadsheet and database programs. CorelCHART is an object linking and embedding server (OLE), so you can embed or link charts into other documents. And it supports dynamic data exchange, so you can build data links with existing spreadsheet files created in other DDE-compatible applications.

CorelMOVE

CorelMOVE gives you the ability to create both simple and complex animations. The animations you create in CorelMOVE can turn a dull presentation into a spectacular multimedia event. It provides the necessary tools for creating the actors, props, and sound effects, as well as the facilities for compositing or layering multiple animated images and sounds. On the CD-ROM there are over two hundred animated flicks, still cartoons, and libraries of sounds for presentations and animations. Once you've created your animation you can use the CorelPLAYER or Video for Windows to play the animation.

CorelSHOW

CorelSHOW helps you assemble multipage presentations using images from programs such as CorelDRAW, CorelCHART, CorelPHOTO-PAINT, and other programs that support Windows OLE, plus animation files created in CorelMOVE. The presentation might be an automated screen show, a series of slides, or overhead transparencies that will be produced at a graphics arts studio.

CorelMOSAIC

CorelMOSAIC is a visual file manager that allows you to organize, manage, and manipulate your files with ease. It lets you view entire subdirectories of images and allows you to select graphic images visually, rather than by file name only. You can also use CorelMOSAIC to store images in compressed libraries and perform batch operations such as printing and exporting groups of files.

It's almost an understatement to say that CorelDRAW can take care of all of your drawing and graphic needs. It has almost everything you could think of or want.

CorelDRAW. Corel Corporation, 1600 Carling Avenue, Ottawa Ontario, Canada K1Z8R7; 800-836-3729. Suggested retail price: $595.

Add Some Life to Your Documents

With Scaleable Fonts You Can Create Thousands of Special Typefaces

Would you like to create letters, memos, faxes, and presentations that make a big impression, have impact, and get you results? Do it with different styles of typefaces and different sizes of fonts.

Let me define a few of the terms used to describe the appearance of text on a printed page. A *typeface* is a family of letters, digits, and characters designed with a distinctive pattern. The term *font* refers to three elements: typeface (e.g., Times Roman, Helvetica), weight (e.g., bold, italic), and point size (e.g., 12 points. A point is ½ of an inch in height). Here is an example of the Helvetica typeface, printed in four different weights and point sizes:

Helvetica Roman, 8 Point

Helvetica Italic, 15 Point

Helvetica Bold, 18 Point

Helvetica Bold Italic, 21 Point

The term *scaleable font* or *scaleable typeface* refers to the ability of the typeface to change sizes, for example:

from Extra-Large

to Large,

to small,

to fine.

So when you're creating a letter, document, or presentation, what kind of impression would you like to make? You can choose a formal, flashy, casual, conservative, or wild typeface. There are liter-

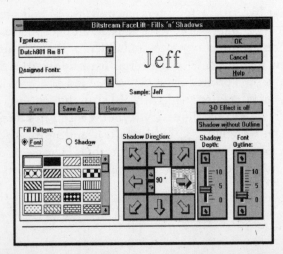

ally hundreds to choose from (Corel Corporation's CorelDRAW comes with 750 different typefaces). Make your selection and tailor your image to suit each situation. And remember, you can use different typefaces interchangeably within your document.

One of the newest features in typeface software allows you to add special effects to any typeface. You select a specific typeface and then choose from a long list of scaleable fill patterns. You can also add three-dimensional shadows, outlines, and backgrounds. For a bold effect, you can even print white type against a black background. These different combinations allow you to create thousands of exciting effects that will add style and impact to all of your documents.

Mr. Neat Mr. Neat

Mr. Neat Mr. Neat

Mr. Neat Mr. Neat

And once you've selected a typeface, you can change its size. You can create letters, numbers, and symbols that are

very small, or

very large.

You can even create letters that are two, four, or six inches high. And best of all, with Windows, you can use every typeface—even the ones you created yourself—with any application.

Facelift for Windows. Bitstream Inc., 215 First Street, Cambridge, MA 02142; 800-522-3668. Suggested retail price: $99.

TrueEffects for Windows. MicroLogic Software, 1351 Ocean Avenue, Emmeryville, CA 94608; 800-888-9078. Suggested retail price: $59.95.

Put the Expertise of a Graphics Designer at Your Fingertips

If you would like to put the expertise of a graphics designer at your fingertips, you'll love By Design. By Design contains a vast library of graphics—hundreds of images in total—that will make your documents, letters, reports, and presentations more upbeat and lively. There are design tools that can help you highlight and enhance your text. You can create different styles for your headers, footers, and page numbering. And there are more than fifty page designs that provide sophisticated graphic layouts for an assortment of business and personal documents ranging from customized letterheads and résumés to title pages, newsletters, and fax cover sheets.

With By Design, you can create professional documents that will get attention in a matter of minutes. By Design is presently available for WordPerfect for DOS, WordPerfect for Windows, and Word for Windows.

By Design. Streetwise Software, 2210 Wilshire Boulevard, Santa Monica, CA 90403; 800-743-6765. Suggested retail price: $69.

Make an Impression with Your Paper

The final step in making your document, presentation, newsletter, or flier look great comes when you print it on the right paper. Paper Direct offers a wide selection of top-quality papers for laser and ink jet printers that will make anything you print stand out. To add personality to your daily correspondence, you can choose from thirteen different personal and business letterhead designs. And there's a wide selection of multicolored, eye-catching, *framed* papers, with matching envelopes, that can be used for letterhead, announcements, signs, invitations, and brochures. They even carry Desktop ColorFoil that turns your laser printer's black type into color print.

Paper Direct. 205 Chubb Avenue, Lyndhurst, NJ 07071. For a catalog call 800-272-3777.

Add Flexibility to Your Printing

Take Control of Your Printer

If you've ever become frustrated with the limitations of your print manager, you'll like what PrintQ has to offer. PrintQ is a collection of eleven utilities that give you enhanced control over your printing output. This is a summary of PrintQ's features:

- You can run, stop, start, and maintain control of up to eight printers simultaneously and continue using your computer while your documents are being printed.
- You can change the order of your print jobs. If you've got a rush job, you can move it ahead of all the others. With this feature you can also reduce the number of times you have to change the paper in your printer tray. You can print all of your letters at one time and then print your invoices, presentations, or proposals. You can even specify a date and time of day that you want your documents to be printed.
- When you need to print multiple copies of a document, you can save time by letting PrintQ, rather than your application, print the additional copies.
- You can view the contents of a print file prior to printing.
- You can print a document even when the computer isn't connected to a printer. This feature is very popular with mobile computer users. It allows them to print their files to disk. When they get back to the office, all they have to do is attach their laptop, notebook, or palmtop to the printer and push the PRINT button.

PrintQ makes it easy for anyone to enjoy faster printing. Simply press a Hot Key, or double click the PrintQ icon, and you'll instantly see the status of all your print jobs and for all your printers.

PrintQ. Software Directions, Inc., 1572 Sussex Turnpike, Randolph, NJ 07869; 800-346-7638. Suggested retail price: $149.

Printing Labels One at a Time Can Now Be Fun

If you've ever printed labels from your laser printer, you know that it's easy to print a whole page of them. But what do you do when you need to print just one label? And how do you print labels for your file folders, boxes, computer diskettes, and name tags? I hope you're not still using a typewriter, or, worse yet, writing them by hand. If you are, I've got a better idea. Use a label printer. Seiko's Smart Label Printer PRO does the job easily and effortlessly.

SLP Pro quickly prints laser-quality labels on a variety of label sizes, incorporating text, photolike graphics, and bar codes. So get rid of your typewriter and use your computer to type all of your labels. You'll save yourself hours of time.

Printing address labels for your letters is a lot of fun because the SLP Pro finds the address for you. Click on the icon and the software searches your document, looking for a block of text that meets all the criteria of an address. When the address is found, it's *captured* and imported into SLP Pro for instant printing. Blocks of highlighted text can also be captured for printing.

SLP Pro makes it easy for you to design your own label format. With a few clicks of the mouse, you decide where on the label the main address and return address is to be positioned and what style and size font you wish to use. You can also include graphic images, special messages, and bar codes.

Once you create a label, the format can be saved in a library. When you need to use the format again, you don't have to create it from scratch. If you want to print your mailing list as labels, just import the list into SLP Pro and click the PRINT button.

Smart Label Printer Pro. Seiko Instruments USA Inc., 1130 Ringwood Court, San Jose, CA 95131; 800-888-0817. Suggested retail price: $299.95.

Print Your Letters and Envelopes at the Same Time

Let me ask you a personal question. Do you find the task of printing envelopes, postcards, and labels a challenging experience? I know that it's easy to print one envelope, but what do you do when you've got to print ten, twenty, or even fifty? If you feed them into your laser printer one at a time, you're not being very productive or efficient. And if you're printing gummed labels and then putting them on your envelopes, you're adding another time-consuming step to the process. Furthermore, sticking a gummed label to a business envelope makes the letter look more like a solicitation for a charitable contribution than important business correspondence.

CoStar offers a very simple solution to this problem. They've developed special envelope printers—the AddressWriter and Address Express—that are designed to work on stand-alone computers or on a network. They print stacks of envelopes, postcards, and pin-feed labels (with the optional label feeder) at once, making it easy to print envelopes, postcards, and labels—one at a time, by the handful, or by the hundreds.

With CoStar's software, you can design your own envelope lay-outs in any size, format, or style. This includes the position of the main address, return address, and any special messages you want to add. To give your envelopes a more distinctive look and get immediate attention, you can import graphic images and you can print bar codes.

The Address Book offers an ideal way for you to manage your mailing lists. You can import and export name and address information from any database or personal information manager, allowing you to print large numbers of envelopes at once.

CoStar's software has special envelope printing features designed to work with any document or letter created in Word for Windows, WordPerfect for Windows, or Ami Pro. When you print your letter on your main printer, the software automatically searches for and captures the letter's address. It then prints the envelope on the envelope printer at the same time your letter is being printed on your main printer. If you send out a lot of correspondence, this can be a wonderful time-saver.

AddressWriter is a dot-matrix printer that prints up to six envelopes or twenty-nine labels per minute. Its small design, 8.7 inches high by 8.5 inches wide by 8 inches deep, lets it fit easily into any cluttered office. Address Express is a thermal inkjet printer capable of printing up to four envelopes per minute. Both hold one hundred envelopes or two hundred postcards, which makes them ideal for printing one envelope at a time—or an entire mailing list.

> **AddressWriter.** CoStar Corporation, 100 Field Point Road, Greenwich, CT 06830; 800-426-9700. Suggested retail price: $399.

> **Address Express.** CoStar Corporation, 100 Field Point Road, Greenwich, CT 06830; 800-426-9700. Suggested retail price: $795.

Add ZIP + 4 to All Your Addresses and Get Better Mail Delivery

DAZzle is a utility program that makes it easy for you to design and print envelopes, labels, and flyers on any size of paper. With the click of the mouse you select where you want the return and main address-

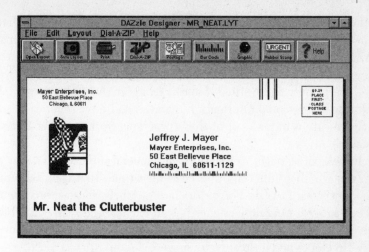

es to appear. Then you can import graphic images, include messages, and add POSTNET bar codes.

The beauty of the program is a feature called Dial-A-ZIP. Many software programs will print a barcode along with the address, but the POSTNET (Postal Numeric Encoding Technique) bar code requires the nine-digit ZIP code (ZIP + 4 in postal speak), which identifies the destination of the mailing piece: the zip code, delivery point, and carrier route. The presence of the POSTNET bar code is important because your letter will be handled with electronic sorting equipment and, you hope, be processed faster and more efficiently.

For many people, it's difficult to obtain the ZIP + 4 zip code. DAZzle eliminates this problem with Dial-A-ZIP. Once you've typed an address or imported it into DAZzle using the Windows clipboard, DAZzle's Dial-A-ZIP dials into a ZIP Station, a remote CD-ROM directory of every address in the United States. Once it makes a connection, it gets the ZIP + 4 zip code and adds it to the address on your envelope. The whole process takes about twenty seconds. Now when you print your envelope, you're printing the POSTNET barcode along with it. (If you send out more than 250 pieces of mail in a single mailing, you can get a substantial discount on the cost of postage with POSTNET bar codes.)

I've had a lot of fun using DAZzle in conjunction with my word processor, personal information manager, SLP Printer Pro, and

AddressWriter. When I want to send a letter, I import the address from my word processor or personal information manager into DAZzle and use Dial-A-ZIP to get the ZIP + 4 zip code. Then the address information is automatically captured by either the label or envelope printer and printed. Finally, I import the ZIP + 4 zip code back into my personal information manager so I have it permanently on file. With Windows, all of these programs work together in harmony.

Envelope Manager Software makes several different versions of DAZzle, which prints only one label at a time. Its suggested retail price is $39.95. DAZzle Plus prints lists of labels. Its suggested retail price is $79.95. DAZzle Designer has all the features of DAZzle Plus and includes special features that make it easy to design business reply envelopes and postcards. Its suggested retail price is $129.95.

Envelope Manager Software also makes a DOS-based program, Envelope Manager, that features all of the formatting, ZIP + 4 barcoding, and printing capabilities of DAZzle and has a database that can handle any size mailing list. With Envelope Manager's Dial-A-ZIP you can look up a hundred ZIP + 4's per call. Its suggested retail price is $79.95.

Envelope Manager Software. 247 High Street, Palo Alto, CA 94301; 800-576-3279.

Let Your Computer Write Your Checks and Balance Your Checking Account

There are several things in life that almost everybody hates to do. They hate to pay bills. They hate the task of trying to balance their checking account. And they hate the process of organizing their financial records so they can prepare their tax returns.

Quicken is a computer program that takes some of the pain and discomfort out of paying bills and keeping accurate financial records. It lets you automate the entire process of taking care of your finances—from paying your bills to keeping track of your invest-

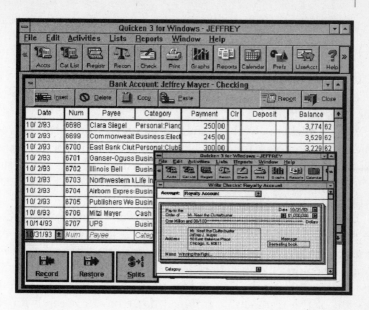

ments to organizing your financial information before preparing your tax returns.

Some people have found that Quicken alone was a reason to go out and purchase a computer, and I'm in total agreement with them. I've been a Quicken user for years. Quicken has saved me hours of time as well as lots of money. (My accountant now prepares my tax return in a fraction of the time it used to take him.) It's a great program.

If I may, I would like to tell you what Quicken's done for me. It's allowed me to automate the whole process of writing checks and keeping track of the balances in my checking and saving accounts. At the end of each month, I'm able to reconcile my statements to the penny—in just a few minutes. I also use Quicken to keep track of my investments in stocks, bonds, and mutual funds. Every time I make a mortgage payment, it recalculates the outstanding balance. It even gives me a place to record the annual increases in the cash value of my life insurance policies. But, most important, Quicken has dramatically reduced the amount of time it takes me to pay my monthly bills as well as helping me to keep very thorough and detailed financial records.

Look at how much wasted time and effort goes into writing checks. First you write a check, then you make an entry into the check register. In some cases, you also write the payee's name and address on an envelope. You've written the payee's name two or three times and the date and the amount of the check twice. Wasted time. Wasted effort.

With Quicken, I've been able to automate the entire process. When I write a check to a new payee, Quicken memorizes the name and mailing address. When the check is printed, the name and address is included. I put the check into a window envelope, add a postage stamp, and I'm done.

Every month I send payments to the same companies. There's the phone and electric bill, the mortgage, several credit cards, etc. To make my life easier, I've created a "transaction group." This is a group of memorized transactions for the people and companies that I send payments to on the first and fifteenth of every month. With the creation of the transaction groups, I don't have to search for the names of the people I've got to send a payment to. At bill-paying time—Quicken reminds me that it's time to pay my bills—I select the transaction group, and the entire list of payees is entered into the check register. All I've got to do is enter the amount of the check. If the amount of my payment is the same each month, like my mortgage payment, it will be automatically entered at the same time the payee's name is entered in the check register. When I've finished writing my checks, I print the checks on my laser printer, three at a time, add my signature, and slide each check into a window envelope.

The great thing about Quicken is that I don't have to write anything longhand. I don't have to write a check. I don't have to make an entry in the check register. And I don't have to address an envelope.

Quicken comes with a complete list of predefined categories and subcategories—automobile, utilities, mortgage, charitable contributions, etc. If you would like to create your own list of categories—I decided to use the same income and expense categories as my accountant—it's easy to do.

Whenever I have a new payee to add to my Quicken account, I

assign it to a specific income or expense category before I memorize the transaction. Every person or company that I have ever written a check to, or received a check from, has been assigned to a specific category. Because of this, I can analyze in detail where my money came from and where it went. And when tax time comes all I've got to do is print a report of my different Quicken accounts, and, within a few minutes, I've got everything I need to have my tax returns prepared.

This feature alone has saved me hours of work. I just print a report, and I've got a detailed analysis of my income and expenses for the entire year. In fact, I even memorized the layout of my reports, so I don't have to set them up again. Since these reports are laid out in a format identical to my accountant's, the amount of time it takes him to prepare my tax returns has been significantly reduced. If you prepare your own taxes, Quicken's financial information can easily be exported into any of the popular tax preparation programs. Quicken is available in DOS, Windows, and Macintosh versions.

Quicken. Intuit, P. O. Box 3014, Menlo Park, CA 94026; 800-624-6095. Suggested retail price: $69.95.

If You Run a Small Business, You Need an Easy-to-Use Accounting Program

If you own a small business, you'll find Quicken's QuickBooks to be very helpful. QuickBooks is a DOS-based product that can help you take care of all your financial record keeping. You can use it to write your checks, keep your check register, create and print your invoices, show the aging of your accounts receivable, and keep track of your accounts payable. QuickBooks can also handle your payroll, write and print your payroll checks, and provide most of the information you need in order to complete your payroll tax forms.

QuickBooks keeps a balance sheet showing all of your assets, liabilities, and net worth. And you can create income and expense reports and cash flow reports. Everything that's associated with your business can be printed as a list—your payees, customers, vendors, employees, projects, and more.

QuickBooks. Intuit, P. O. Box 3014, Menlo Park, CA 94026; 800-624-6095. Suggested retail price: $139.95.

Spend Your Valuable Time Analyzing Your Spreadsheets Instead of Building Them

Would you like to be able to view your spreadsheet information from many different perspectives? Would you like a spreadsheet that allows you to write formulas in plain English—"gross profit = (total sales * price) – cost of goods sold"—instead of in cryptic code, "B5 = (B2 * B3) – B4"? Would you like a spreadsheet that allows you to change your graph or chart from one type to another just by pointing and clicking a button on the mouse? If so, you've got to take a look at Lotus's new spreadsheet, Improv. Improv is unlike any spreadsheet you've ever seen before. With its revolutionary new approach, you

		Chicago	New York	Los Angeles	Total Sales
	January	100	201	175	476
Widgits	February	125	195	148	468
	March	98	228	182	508
	Three Month	323	624	505	1452
	January	332	178	415	925
Watchamacallits	February	298	193	428	919
	March	378	219	398	995
	Three Month	1008	590	1241	2839
	January	422	400	322	1144
Thingamajigs	February	501	472	349	1322
	March	475	428	337	1240
	Three Month	1398	1300	1008	3706

1 Three Month Totals = January + February + March

2 Total Sales:Three Month Totals:Widgits = Chicago:January:Widgits +Chicago:February:Widgits +Chicago:March:Widgits +New York:January:Widgits +New York:February:Widgits +New York:March:Widgits +Los Angeles:January:Widgits +Los Angeles:February:Widgits +Los Angeles:March:Widgits
Overlaps formula 1

can use your mouse to view and analyze the same information in many different ways.

Items and Categories

An Improv spreadsheet does not use the traditional rows and columns. Instead it uses *items* and *categories*. An item is a unit of information whose location in the spreadsheet is not fixed. This flexibility allows you to rearrange the spreadsheet data. In one view of a spreadsheet an item may appear in a row, in another, the same item will appear in a column.

For example, items across the top of an Improv spreadsheet could be the months of the year—January, February, etc.—and the items down the side could be the name of the products sold—"Widgets," "Watchamacallits," and "Thingamajigs." The point where the two items, months and sales, intersect forms a *cell*. A cell is used to store manually entered data or data that was calculated in a formula. In this example, the values in each cell would represent the number of units sold by month. A *category* is a collection of items. When you name a category you clarify how you've organized your information. In this example, the names of the two categories would be "Year" and "Products."

The beauty of Improv is that by using the mouse to drag a category from one position on a spreadsheet to another you can change the view of the spreadsheet. When you move a category, the data moves too, giving you different views of the same data. These multiple views let you look at that same set of data in a variety of ways, thereby eliminating the need to rebuild a spreadsheet, reenter data, or copy formulas.

Formulas

In Improv, formulas are written in plain English—"gross profit = (total sales * price) − cost of goods sold"—and are associated with items, not cells. So it isn't necessary to rewrite a formula when the view of a spreadsheet is changed. The days of writing cryptic formulas that are associated with specific cells—"B5 = (B2 * B3) − B4"—are over. Since the formulas are written in English, even the most sophisticated spreadsheets are easy to read and understand.

Creating a formula is easy. You create the formula by pointing and clicking your categories and the Formula Bar, which has all the mathematical functions, with the mouse. Formulas are easy to read and understand because you use item names—the names you've chosen to build your spreadsheet—in the formula. Once numbers are inserted in each cell the formula automatically calculates and displays the results. A single formula can calculate the values in many cells.

Charts and Graphs

With the click of a mouse you can create a chart from your spreadsheet data. Improv offers more than twenty different types of charts and graphs—including three-dimensional bar charts and pie charts—to choose from. And you can change from one type of chart or graph to another simply by clicking the Chart Bar with your mouse. As your spreadsheet data changes, the graphs and charts are automatically updated.

If you're in a business where you need to look at your data from many different points of view, Improv can save you a lot of time. Just click the mouse and you can instantly redesign the layout of your spreadsheet. With Improv you'll be spending less time building spreadsheets and more time analyzing the data that's critical to your business.

Improv. Lotus Development Corporation, 55 Cambridge Parkway, Cambridge, MA 02142; 800-343-5414. Suggested retail price: $495.

Increase Your Productivity by Using Macros

One of the easiest ways you can increase your productivity is by using macros. A macro, also called a *script,* is a feature in almost every computer software program. As previously noted, it allows you to record a series of keystrokes and works in the same way as the redial feature on your telephone. The macro is activated by typing a few keystrokes. Then, the entire series of recorded keystrokes is replayed.

Years ago, typing competitions were held on a regular basis. The winner was the person who could type the fastest with the fewest mistakes. Today, I think there should be a macro contest. The winner would be the person who could write the most useful macros, because a computer can execute keyboard commands and type keystrokes much faster and with more accuracy than any human.

The use of macros can also reduce the possibility of sustaining a repetitive stress injury. By allowing the computer to automate repetitive commands, the typing of sentences or phrases, you are significantly reducing the number of keystrokes you type during a day. I'll be discussing more ways to avoid repetitive stress injuries in Part IV, Winning the Fight Between You and Your Body.

The use of macros falls into two distinct categories. One is keyboard commands, and the other is frequently used phrases. To best illustrate how macros work, I would like to tell you about some of the macros I use. Since I'm an author, the majority of my keyboard time is spent using my word processing software, WordPerfect. In WordPerfect, I've created a number of macros that make the writing of books, letters, and other correspondence much easier.

Let me give you a few examples. When I write a chapter or sub-chapter heading, I want the heading to be capitalized and bold-faced, and I want a set of codes for the table of contents inserted at the beginning and ending of the heading. These three separate formatting tasks take a lot of time and require many keystrokes. When the same set of keyboard commands are being done over and over again, it represents a great deal of wasted time and energy. After having created several hundred headings, I asked myself, Why didn't I write a macro that did this?

Through trial and error and several calls to WordPerfect's technical support, I created a macro, called TOC, that does exactly what I want. It works in three separate stages. First, the heading is capitalized, then bold-faced, and, finally, just before the codes that mark the beginning and the ending of the table of contents are inserted, the macro pauses. This allows me to designate which level I want to assign—1, 2, or 3—to this heading in the table of contents. I make my selection, press ENTER, and the macro continues to completion. The whole process takes less than a second.

With time I found that using the normal macro command, ALT + F10 + TOC, to be too much of a bother (look at how far I had come), so I assigned the macro to the CTRL + T key in my custom keyboard. (I couldn't assign it to ALT + T because I use that to change my tab settings.) So by pressing just two keys, instead of two plus three, I can have the macro execute a series of formatting commands that would take me at least sixty seconds, and many keystrokes, to do myself.

One feature that I use all the time is the view document screen. This lets me see what my document will look like on a printed page, (at the moment I'm still using WordPerfect 5.1). To save myself a few keystrokes, I created a macro, ALT + V, that took me directly to the view document screen. I know I only reduced three keystrokes to two, but most important, I no longer have to search for any keys. I always knew where to find the ALT + V key.

One day I was reading *WordPerfect the Magazine* (800-228-9626), and read a story about the winners of a recent competition that the magazine had sponsored. The theme of the contest was who can write the best macro. One of the winners wrote a brilliant macro. Whenever I use it, I feel as if I'm being beamed up to the starship *Enterprise*.

This macro takes the user to the view document screen and back again—from almost anywhere within WordPerfect. If I'm making a change to a header or footer and want to see how the changes look, I press ALT + V and am instantly transported to the view document screen. When I press exit, I'm returned to my header or footer. This also works from the graphics images screen. When I'm editing, sizing, or positioning an image, I often want to see how it's positioned on the page. I press ALT + V and am once again transported to the view document screen. When I exit, I'm sent back to the graphics editor, where I can make additional changes. I can't begin to tell you how many keystrokes I've saved by using this macro, nor can I estimate how much time it has saved me. But it's sure a lot of fun to use.

In addition, I've created macros that check the spelling of my documents and macros that create my table of contents. One day a portion of this manuscript was returned to me by an editor and I found that he had removed the majority of the commas that I had inserted. So I created a macro that looked for commas. This made it easier for me to locate and remove the ones that he felt weren't needed.

I use the majority of my macros for the purpose of automating keyboard commands. You can create macros that will insert frequently used paragraphs, phrases, or the openings and closings of your letters. If you frequently send out correspondence to the same people, you could create a macro that inserts the date, name, address, greeting, and closing. If you have standard paragraphs that you use over and over again, you can record a macro that will insert them into your documents.

Anything you do repetitively should be recorded as a macro. I've got friends who've created macros that sort their databases and crunch the numbers on their spreadsheets. You can even write a macro that will automate your backup program. The use of macros will certainly make you more productive and help you improve the quality of your work. We're paid to get the job done. When you're using a macro you can get the job done quicker, faster, and better.

Create Eye-catching Charts, Graphs, and Tables with the Click of Your Mouse

Presenting information is something we all do every day. Sometimes we're preparing a status report for the other members of our work group. Or maybe we're preparing a report that will bring our boss up-to-date on our work. Other times, we may find ourselves standing in front of a group of people using a slide or overhead projector.

Whenever you're meeting with someone, you'll probably need to make a handout that will include a graph, table, chart, or other piece of information. And if you're giving a speech, you'll probably need speaker notes to go along with each slide or overhead transparency.

To make the presentation of your information look good, you need a presentation program like WordPerfect Presentations. WordPerfect Presentations is a comprehensive software package that gives you all the tools you need to create, organize, and manage the presentation of information. You can use WP Presentations to design and create charts, graphs, drawings, and illustrations that can be used to make professional slide shows, overhead transparencies, handouts for meetings, or any other type of information that you would present on paper. WordPerfect Presentations is so easy to use that in just a matter of minutes you can create presentations that have impact and get results.

Create Any Type of Chart

Do you need a chart? With WordPerfect Presentations, you can have any kind you want: a bar chart, a bullet chart, a line chart, a table chart, a pie chart, an area chart, a surface chart, a high-low chart, or a scatter chart. Your charts can be flat or three-dimensional.

To create your chart you can either import your financial or statistical information from your spreadsheet program into WordPerfect Presentation's unique split-screen editor or enter it yourself into WordPerfect Presentations's spreadsheet. The split-screen editor displays the spreadsheet at the top of the screen and the chart on the bottom half. As you edit information in the spreadsheet, the changes are immediately reflected in the chart. If you decide that you want a different type of chart, all you've got to do is click on the desired chart with your mouse and the new chart will be instantly displayed.

When you're finished making your chart you can position it anywhere you want on the page and can change the chart's size, colors, and fill patterns with just a few clicks of the mouse. Once the chart's been placed where you want it, with another click of the mouse you can add titles and text. You can choose from more than fifty styles of scaleable fonts.

Edit Your Graphic Images

WordPerfect Presentations comes with more than a thousand pieces of colorful and editable clip art. You can use these graphic images in any of your slides or presentation pieces. With the click of a mouse, you can change the image's size, position, orientation, and colors. Once you've edited a graphic image or created one of your own from scratch, it can be saved in any of eight popular graphics formats.

Draw Your Own Images

WordPerfect Presentations contains one of the most comprehensive set of drawing tools in the presentation graphics market. You can draw lines, curves, ellipses, rectangles, and more. You can even draw freehand. Once you create your drawing, you can select different colors and fill patterns and even change the thickness and color of the lines. You can also edit bit-mapped images in the bit map editor.

Scanning

You can scan images into WordPerfect Presentations that can then be edited pixel-by-pixel with the bit map editor.

Creating Slides Is Easy

When you create presentation material, everything is done with the click of the mouse. This allows you to concentrate on the content of the page rather than on its layout or format. The process for creating presentation material is the same for every medium you may be using: printed material, overhead transparencies, or 35mm slides. You can also have the computer give the presentation by itself. The only difference is how the computer file is processed once the presentation material has been created.

You begin by selecting a background template. There are dozens of formats and hundreds of colors you can choose. To the background you then add charts, drawings, graphic images, text, and titles. (It took me longer to install the program, which ships on ten floppy disks and takes up 22 megabytes of disk space, than it took me to make my first slide.)

Once you've created your slides, you select the order in which you want them to appear. You then add the transition slides that will give your presentation an even flow. This way you advance gracefully from one slide to the next.

Add Sound to Your Slide Shows

Sound increases the impact of any presentation. With a sound card, you can add special sound effects, music, or a recording of your own voice to your slide presentation. There are three different types of sound files you can use:

- **Digital Audio.** You can use the Windows Sound Recorder to record any sound or your voice and include it as a part of your slide show. These files are called Wave files, from the file's extension *.WAV. It is any type of recording that comes from an external sound feed such as a microphone, a compact disc, or a CD-ROM.
- **Compact Disk.** You can record music from a compact disc or from a CD-ROM.
- **MIDI.** A MIDI file (Musical Instrument Digital Interface) is created from a computer-based synthesizer. It is a system for re-creating musical sounds. With the proper software you can compose your own MIDI music. More than a hundred MIDI sound clips come with WordPerfect Presentations.

When you add sound to your slide show, you have the flexibility to decide when you want the sound clip to start and how long you want it to run. This way, you can change the mood and feeling of your presentation as you progress from one slide to the next. Once you've created your slide show presentation, you can change from one slide to the next manually or have the computer play the slide show for you.

Link Your Presentation to Other Applications

With object linking and embedding (OLE), WordPerfect Presentations can act as an OLE server and create objects (drawings, illustrations, charts, graphics, or other elements) that can be linked or embedded into any Windows client application. And as an OLE client, WordPerfect Presentations supports OLE server applications. With OLE, video clips can also be inserted into your drawings or slides.

Almost anything that has to do with the presentation of information can be created by WordPerfect Presentations. You can also create business forms, fliers, flowcharts, and organizational charts. With the drawing capabilities, you can create advertisements, large banners, and design maps. I've even found some additional uses for WordPerfect Presentations.

I used WordPerfect Presentations to create all the illustrations that are used in this book. I would take a "snapshot" of a Windows application by pressing ALT + PRINTSCREEN, which would copy the image to the Windows Clipboard and would then import it into WordPerfect Presentations for editing. The image would be resized to a five-by-seven format, and a border would be added, if needed. For a few of the images, I took a second or third "snapshot," resized it, and made an overlay over the first image.

Once I had laid out the image in a format that I liked, I would print it to file using a Linotronic 330 as the printer. A Linotronic is a special graphics printer that prints at 1,200 dots per square inch. The printer driver comes with Microsoft Windows. However, I don't own one. So I would print the images to file, copy the print file to a floppy disk, and take it to a local graphic arts studio, where they would print my images on their Linotronic.

One of the unexpected benefits of having WordPerfect Presentations is that it keeps my three-year-old daughter occupied for hours. WordPerfect Presentations comes with a collection of clip art animal images. I'm frequently making pictures of dogs, cats, horses, and cows, in different sizes, shapes, and orientations. I print out five or ten copies at a time, and DeLaine has a field day coloring them with crayons or watercolors. And she always gets a big thrill when the picture comes out of the printer.

WordPerfect Presentations. WordPerfect Corporation, 1555 N. Technology Way, Orem, UT 84057; 800-451-5151. Suggested retail price: $495.

Bring Your Computer into Your Business Meetings and Throw away Your Slides and Overhead Transparencies

For most of us, meetings are a very important part of our lives. And in today's high-tech world, we do all our planning and preparation for those meetings at a computer. Yet when we go into the meeting, we're often giving the presentation with the aid of an overhead projector, 35mm slides, or paper handouts. So here's a great idea: Instead of taking those computer files and turning them into overhead transparencies or 35mm slides, just bring the computer into the meeting! With Desktop Projection from Proxima, you can use your computer to make your presentation.

A desktop projector is a small lightweight liquid crystal display projection panel that sits on top of an overhead projector and is connected to the computer with a cable. The projection panel captures any image that would appear on the computer's monitor—spreadsheets, charts, graphs, project schedules, document outlines, animated graphics, illustrations, and even video images—and displays them on-screen through the overhead projector.

With a desktop projector and a computer, you can turn the old-fashioned overhead projector into a powerful interactive communication tool. You now have the ability not only to make last-minute changes, but you can even change your presentation material on the fly, manipulate your data in real time, explore "what if . . . " scenarios, and display the results instantly. With Desktop Projection, you have no slides, no transparencies, and no presentation headaches.

Turn Your Pointer into a Cordless Mouse

Once you begin using your computer to present your ideas in meetings and before audiences, you'll find that you prefer to be standing in front of your audience instead of sitting behind the computer. With Cyclops, which functions like a cordless mouse, you can turn the projection screen into one big interactive monitor. Cyclops allows you to open files, select menu items, and navigate through presentations by pointing and clicking at the projected image.

Desktop Projection and Cyclops. Proxima Corporation, 6610 Nancy Ridge Drive, San Diego, CA 92121. Proxima Corporation offers a complete line of LCD projection panels, and the Cyclops interactive pointer system. Call 800-447-7694 for product information and a list of current prices.

Add Sound to Your Computer

If you really want to make an impression with both your computer presentations, modem, or E-mail communications, add sound to your computer files! With a sound card, you can add music and speech to your list of computer tools. But before I go any further, I would like to take a quick moment and explain how a sound card works. Basically, it allows you to record and play sounds from your computer as if it were a tape recorder. The older sound cards recorded in 8-bit segments and a sampling rate of 11kHz. The sampling rate is a measure of how often sound is converted from an analog waveform to digital numbers. This is okay for recording a person's voice but isn't very good for reproducing music, because the quality of sound is about the same as you would get from a cheap FM radio.

The new sound cards record in 16-bit segments and use a sampling rate of 44kHz. These are the same standards that are used in the recording of musical compact discs, and they provide a measure of how closely a recorded sound matches the original sound source when it is played back.

Media Vision, Inc., of Fremont, California, is a leader in sound card technology. Their Pro AudioStudio 16 sound card is one of the most advanced sound cards on the market. It records in 16-bit stereo and has a built-in twenty-voice Yamaha synthesizer so you can compose your own MIDI music. It also has a built-in connection for a CD-ROM drive, so if you want to add one at a later time, you don't have to use up a second expansion slot. And best of all, they offer toll-free technical support from Monday through Friday 6:00 A.M. to 8:00 P.M. (PST), and on Saturday and Sunday from 8:00 A.M. to 4:00 P.M. (PST). I found this to be very helpful. I installed my Media Vision sound card and CD-ROM on a Saturday and had to call technical support two or three times before I was able to get everything to work as it was supposed to.

The Pro AudioStudio 16 comes bundled with some of the most advanced Windows sound software on the market today. It has Monologue, ExecuVoice, Recording Session, and Sound Editor, which I'll be discussing on the following pages. If you already own a Media Vision sound card and would like to purchase the above-mentioned software, it's available in their Pro Audio PowerPak for $79.

Pro AudioStudio 16. Media Vision, Inc., 47300 Bayside Parkway, Fremont, CA 94538; 800-845-5870. Suggested retail price: $349.

Add Sound to Your Documents, Letters, and Presentations

Once you've added a sound card to your computer, you can add voice, or any recorded sound, to your documents with the object linking and embedding (OLE) feature. When you *embed* a sound file into a document, you're importing all the information about the sound file into the document. So when you're writing a letter or memo that you're going to send over your electronic mail network, you can now add a voice message. To do so, you click on the edit menu and select Insert Object, which in this case would be your sound recorder, and the program is launched. You then record your message, save the file, and an icon is placed in your document as a representation of the recording. To play the recording just double click the icon.

Once this *embedded object* has become a part of your file, you can do anything you want with it. If you want to append the file to an electronic mail message or send the file via modem to someone else, they not only can read the text when it's received, but they can also listen to your comments by double clicking the sound icon. So when you want to make a point, or explain something in greater detail, it's no longer necessary to write everything out. You can record your thoughts and comments and include them as part of your electronic correspondence.

There are some other interesting, and productivity improving, things you can do once you add a sound card to your computer. In addition to recording your own voice, you can have the computer read your documents or electronic mail to you, you can control the computer with voice commands instead of keyboard commands, and you can even speak into a microphone and have your words turned into edited text that appears in your Windows word processor.

Have Your Computer Read Your Documents out Loud

You can now add the power of speech to your repertoire of productivity-improving Windows applications. Monologue 16 for Windows is a speech synthesizer that gives any application that includes written text the ability to speak the data. Monologue 16 can do the following to help you become more productive:

- Monologue can proofread your documents. You no longer have to hold the printed page next to the computer screen. You have the computer read the text while you read the document and make any notations for corrections or changes.
- If you've got to check the accuracy of numbers that were entered into a computer spreadsheet, Monologue will read the computer's numbers out loud while you compare them to your worksheet.
- If you need to compare the information you've entered into a database with the original list, Monologue will read the fields in your database.
- You can have Monologue read your electronic mail while you're doing something else. You no longer have to read each message yourself, which can become a rather time-consuming task.

By adding voice power, your ears can complement the productivity of your eyes and hands. When proofreading a letter, presentation, or report, it's very easy to miss a grammatical mistake. Words are accidentally omitted or are transposed, and occasionally important parts of speech or grammar are used incorrectly.

Many times I'll read my text out loud just so I can hear the flow of my words. When I do, I frequently discover that I had unintentionally omitted or transposed some words or had used some words incorrectly. I also find that I sometimes lose the flow of a sentence even though the words and phrases I've used are grammatically correct. When I hear the sentence out loud, the omission is glaringly evident.

Monologue is easy to use. Just highlight the desired text or selected information, copy it to the Windows Clipboard, and click on the Monologue icon. The contents of the clipboard are immediately retrieved by Monologue, converted to speech, and voice output begins. You can also initiate the direct reading of your text from within your application by utilizing Windows's Dynamic Data Exchange feature. When Monologue is in the Dynamic Data Exchange server mode, Monologue will speak any data sent to it by the other application once a conversation is initiated.

Monologue 16 for Windows is bundled with Media Vision's Pro AudioStudio 16 sound card, their Pro Audio PowerPak, and their Pro 16 Multimedia System.

Control Your Computer by Speaking

Have you ever thought to yourself, It would be nice if I could just speak commands to my computer, instead of using pull-down menus or typing multiple keystrokes. With ExecuVoice's voice-activated software you can use voice commands to start your Windows software applications—WordPerfect, Lotus, dBase, etc.—and, to open a file, scroll through a file, print a file, open another application and then switch to it, and a whole lot more.

ExecuVoice is designed to help you navigate through Windows without using the keyboard. You can execute each and every command of the programs in the Windows Accessories Group by speaking. These include Calculator, Calendar, Cardfile, Clock, Media

Player, Notepad, Terminal, and Write. You can also execute the commands of the File Manager, Program Manager, and Help.

Once you've opened any program, you can use your voice to activate keyboard commands for many of the basic editing functions such as: Enter, Spacebar, Backspace, Help, Tab, Shift Tab, Page Up, and Page Down. You can also use editing commands such as copy, cut, paste, and undo, as well as file commands such as file open, close, new, print, save, and save as.

The more you use ExecuVoice, the more familiar it becomes with your voice as you "train" it to understand how you speak. If ExecuVoice doesn't respond to one of your voice commands, the program will ask you to repeat the word or phrase several times so that it can "refresh" its memory. Within a few moments, it will acknowledge that it understands the word you are saying.

The first time I called up the notepad, the notepad appeared, but when I said "file open" ExecuVoice printed a page instead. By repeating "file open" eight or ten times I *trained* ExecuVoice to respond to the "file open" command. Then the program acknowledged that it understood the command, and I haven't had a problem since.

ExecuVoice comes with a large vocabulary of pretrained voice commands, each corresponding to the menu commands in an application. One of the nice features of ExecuVoice is that you don't have to remember all the available voice commands, because a list of the commands remains visible in an on-screen window.

I enjoy using ExecuVoice because it starts my programs for me. When I've two or more programs running at the same time, I can toggle between them simply by saying, "Swap with . . . " And using ExecuVoice in the Windows File Manager makes locating and working with files easy, since every command is voice activated. For example, I can sort the files within a directory simply by saying, "Sort by . . . date, size, name, type," and it's done. This is much faster than clicking the mouse three or four times. I can also expand and collapse the directory branches just by saying "expand" or "collapse."

ExecuVoice is bundled with Media Vision's Pro AudioStudio 16 sound card, their Pro Audio PowerPak, and their Pro 16 Multimedia System.

Speak into a Microphone and Watch Your Words Appear on Your Computer Screen

If you would like to eliminate the use of the keyboard altogether, it's now possible to speak into a microphone and have your words appear as editable text on the computer screen. With Dragon System's DragonDictate, you can create everything from business memos and letters to complex documents and reports without ever touching the keyboard or clicking the mouse. You simply talk into a microphone, and the computer responds, carrying out your application's commands and displaying your words on the computer screen as they are spoken.

DragonDictate has the ability to control the MS-DOS operating system, the Windows graphical user interface, and the most popular word processing, spreadsheet, and database programs, including Microsoft Word, WordPerfect, Lotus 1-2-3, Quicken, and dBase. DragonDictate can also be used with your LAN, electronic mail, and faxing software.

Speech recognition products were originally developed with the disabled in mind. Today speech-to-text products are now being used by thousands of people in business, manufacturing, health care, law, education, computer programming, finance, and journalism. Here are just a few of the ways speech recognition software is being used today:

- Doctors, lawyers, and other business professionals who frequently dictate memos, letters, notes, and other correspondence into a tape recorder are now dictating the same information directly into the computer. This saves them time and eliminates the need for transcription.
- In situations where users need the use of their hands or eyes to perform other tasks—such as holding, manipulating, or examining objects; leafing through papers or filling out reports— speech input allows them to complete those tasks while simultaneously inputting data.

If a person is not a speed typist or simply prefers not to type, DragonDictate gives them the opportunity to take advantage of the power of their computer. And for the person who has a physical disability or is suffering from a repetitive stress injury, DragonDictate offers much more than a choice about how they want to work with their computer. It may be the only way they can continue to make a living.

The program comes with a large, 30,000-word active vocabulary, and a 120,000-word backup dictionary. You can also add proper names, jargon, or any additional words or phrases that are suited to your specific needs. It's patented speaker-adaptaton features help the program become familiar with your voice, vocabulary, and speaking style.

DragonDictate normally produces voice-to-text output of about thirty-five words a minute, but with voice-activated macros—each macro can generate up to two thousand keystrokes—it's possible to automate the inputting of familiar words and phrases so as to increase this rate to one hundred words per minute. DragonDictate's error correction feature helps it to learn from its mistakes. Each time you say a word that the computer doesn't understand, a box appears on-screen with a list of words that DragonDictate thinks you said, ranked in order of probability. If the word you said appears at the top of the list, you simply continue dictating, giving DragonDictate the go-ahead to enter the word. If none of the possibilities on the choice list match what you said, you just begin spelling it, using the International Communications Alphabet (alpha, bravo, charlie . . . zulu), or type it in. And as you enter text, DragonDictate automatically adds the correct number of spaces after words and at the end of sentences. When it comes to words that sound alike, such as *to*, *too*, *2*, and *Two*, DragonDictate determines the correct word based on probability and context.

Whether you're looking for an alternative to keyboard input or a way to increase the efficiency of your business, you'll find DragonDictate to be a more natural, independent, and productive way to use your computer. It's a dream come true for anyone who cannot or does not want to type. DragonDictate is also available in some European languages—British English and German.

DragonDictate. Dragon Systems, Inc., 320 Nevada Street, Newton, MA 02160; 800-825-5897. Suggested retail price: $4,995.

Make Your Own Computer Music

MIDI (Musical Instrument Digital Interface) was developed in 1983 as a means of allowing synthesizers from different manufacturers to communicate with one another and with the computer. This turned the dream of creating a productive relationship among computers, electronic musical instruments, and musicians into reality. MIDI is the language that electronic musical instruments and computers use to communicate with each other.

Recording Session allows you to record, play, and edit your MIDI musical compositions. You can open any MIDI file and actually see music being played in real time. All the musical notations are displayed on sheet music, along with the different lines for each instrument, for example, trumpet, piano, clarinet, drums, etc. As the music is played, the notes change color, and the current measure is always displayed on screen.

You can compose your own musical compositions just by clicking notes on the sheet music with your mouse. Click on the PLAY button and you can listen to your composition. After you've completed your composition, you can change the selection of instruments with a few clicks of the mouse. If you play an instrument, with the proper equipment, you can play it, and Recording Session will translate the notes

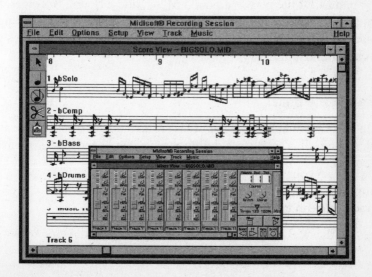

into standard musical notation—in real time—as they are played. If you make a mistake, you can come back later and correct it.

If you're a musician and like to play with other instruments, you can mute the sound track that applies to your instrument and play along "with the band." If you want to purchase additional MIDI files, they are often advertised in computer magazines. In addition, there is a MIDI forum on Compuserve, where you can download compositions of other MIDI composers. I've studied classical piano for many years, and I can only imagine the kind of musical creations a Bach, Brahms, Beethoven, or Mozart could have composed had these tools been available to them. It boggles the mind.

Recording Session is bundled with Media Vision's Pro Audio-Studio 16 sound card, their Pro Audio PowerPak, and their Pro 16 Multimedia System.

Take Control of Your Computer Music and Sound Effects

Sound Impressions—which looks like your familiar home stereo—is a multimedia sound system that allows you to have full control of your sound card's sophisticated features. There is a CD player, a MIDI file player, a Sound Mixer, and a Sound Recorder. Its comprehensive features let you play, record, edit, and mix music, and create sounds from a range of sources. You can even add voice-overs to your sound and music clips.

The Mixing Panel

The Mixing Panel lets you maintain precise control over volume and balance for all components during the playing or recording of music or sound.

Wave Recorder/Player

You use the Wave Recorder/Player just as you would a tape recorder. You select a "*.wav" file and click on the PLAY button. A "wave" is

the popular name for the *.WAV file format, which is any type of recording that comes from an external sound feed: a microphone, compact disc, tape recorder, or other device.

Waveform Editor

Sound Impression's Waveform editor lets you play, record, edit, modify, and add special effects to any existing wave file or newly created waveform. You can add or remove silence from a recording, and with the noise filter, you can "clean it up." You can also add special effects such as Echo, Chorus, Flange, Fade, Pan, and Crossfade to entire sessions or segments and can even switch between mono and stereo.

MIDI Player

Plays single MIDI tunes or batches of them in a continuous loop.

CD Player

With the Compact Disc Player, you can play an audio CD, then turn to any other Windows task and enjoy the sounds of your music in the background. You also have the ability to arrange tracks into play lists that can be stored and later retrieved when you use the same CD.

Object Linking and Embedding

Object linking and embedding (OLE) allows you to transfer any sound file or composition from Sound Impression to any other Windows application capable of receiving OLE data. This enables the destination, or *client*, application to use the data as if it were its own. OLE also enables the client application to call up the source application, the *server*, in order to edit or update data objects. Sound Impression's unique implementation of OLE permits the transfer of any supported sound data—Wave, MIDI, CD, even the current Mixing Panel settings—to an OLE "client" application with just a few clicks or keystrokes.

Creating a link is easy. To link a Sound Impression Wave, MIDI, or CD file to a Windows OLE client application just open a sound file and click on the "links" icon. Then open the application, click on the "paste link" option, and your link appears. Double click your link icon and the sound is replayed. Once the link has been established it can be changed, edited, or deleted.

Add Pictures, Video, and Animation to Your Computer with a CD-ROM

Until you've actually installed a CD-ROM on your computer you can't fully understand, comprehend, or appreciate what it's capable of doing. A CD-ROM merges text, graphics, sound, animation, pictures, and video into what is commonly called multimedia.

The reason CD-ROMs are able to do this is because of their phenomenal ability to store digital information. A compact disc holds about 680 megabytes of data. This represents the capacity of almost 500 floppy disks, or 250,000 pages of print. To give you an idea of their capacity, the twelve-volume *Oxford English Dictionary*, plus the four-volume supplement, fits on a single CD-ROM. The entire *Encyclopaedia Britannica* is stored on two CD-ROMs. Today, CD-ROMs are being used in the business world as a vehicle for storing huge amounts of information or reference data and in the home as an information and educational reference tool as well as an interactive game player.

Here are some of the ways businesses are using the CD-ROM:

- The aircraft maintenance manuals for the Boeing 767 and MD-80 airplanes are on CD-ROM. This includes their illustrated parts catalogs, wiring diagrams, and illustrations. The 767's CD-ROM has more than nine thousand illustrations.
- Equipment manufacturers are putting their service manuals on CD-ROM. When their maintenance people go out to make a service call, they take their laptop computer and a portable CD-ROM with them.
- Many companies are putting their reference manuals on CD-ROM and then making the information available on their network. This makes it easy to update information and eliminates the need to print thousands of manuals that are seldom if ever looked at.

The uses for CD-ROMs are increasing almost every day. Complete road maps of the United States are now available as well as a huge amount of census, statistical, and economic information. If you would like a listing of the 80 million households and 9.6 million businesses in the United States, you can now find it on a single CD-ROM.

Computer software manufacturers are beginning to make their application software available on CD-ROM, in addition to floppy disks, because the programs are becoming too big. WordPerfect Presentations ships on ten floppy disks—taking up 25 megabytes of hard disk space. Quattro Pro takes up almost 20 megabytes of hard disk space. Corel's CorelDRAW now ships with two CD-ROMs that hold 750 fonts and 18,000 pieces of clip art (800-836-3729). Bitstream (800-522-3668) has a CD-ROM that holds all of its fonts. A user can try a typeface, and if he wants to use it he can call a toll-free number, purchase the typeface, and get the authorization code that unlocks the CD-ROM. Walnut Creek CD-ROM (800-786-9907) is a mail order house that offers CD-ROMs packed full of the world's highest quality MS-DOS shareware. This includes disk utilities, screen savers, Microsoft Windows programs, games, and more. Each CD-ROM has more than 9,000 files on it.

In the future, you'll be seeing fully operational versions of major applications such as spreadsheets, word processors, and graphic drawing programs that will be available on a single CD-ROM. These will be inserted in computer magazines, included in the box with a new computer, and spread around the marketplace in many other ways. Potential customers will be allowed to load and run each program for a limited number of times—five or six perhaps—to get an idea of whether or not they like it. If they do, they can call a toll-free number, purchase the software over the phone, and get the password that makes the program fully operational.

A number of software manufacturers are also making their software available on CD-ROM so users won't have to take up so much of their disk space with *another* application. The CD-ROM application is installed just like any other piece of software using the "set up" instructions. The only difference is that all the application's files are stored on the CD-ROM instead of on the computer's hard drive. When you want to use the CD-ROM you put the disc in the player and click on the icon.

Add Brilliant Color Photographs to Your Documents and Presentations

Corel Corporation has created a collection of photo CD-ROMs that each has a hundred royalty-free Kodak Photo-CD color images. (Photo-CD is a process developed by Eastman Kodak Company that converts 35mm film into the digital format and stores them on a CD.) Such themes—as of this writing there are eighty-one titles—include: Arizona Desert, Birds, Fighter Jets, Fireworks, Lamborghinis, Lingerie, Mountains, Sunsets and Sunrises, WWII Aircraft, Water Fowl, and Wild Animals.

These images can be used in everything from advertisements to document cover pages, to business presentations. They can even be used as your Windows Wallpaper—the Windows background that is displayed on your monitor—and as your screen saver, the images that are displayed on your screen when the computer is idle. These photographic images give you a lot of flexibility.

- They can be exported for use in any document or presentation using the TIFF, BMP, EPS, or PCX formats.
- The resolution can be altered from 129 × 192 pixels to 2048 × 3072 pixels.
- They can be reproduced in gray scale, 16 color or 256 color. If you're using a 24-bit video card they can be reproduced in 16 million colors.
- You can include any Photo-CD image in an automatic slide show for viewing on your computer monitor. Seven different types of background music are included.

Corel Professional Photos also come with a CD-Audio player that lets you play music CDs from your CD-ROM drive and CorelMOSAIC, which is an innovative CorelDRAW application designed to display, organize, and manage your graphics files as "thumbnails," small bit-mapped representations of your graphics files. This allows you to select image files visually rather than by file name only.

Corel Professional Photos. Corel Corporation, 1600 Carling Avenue, Ottawa, Ontario, Canada K1Z8R7; 800-772-6735. Suggested retail price: $49.95.

Add Special Sound Effects to Your Presentations and You'll Make a **Big** Impression

If you want to make an impression, bring the latest state-of-the-art sound effects into your multimedia presentations. "1000 of the World's Greatest Sound Effects" features digitally mastered sound effects—recorded in both 8-bit and 16-bit high-fidelity formats—from the renowned Valentino Sound Effects Library. These are the same sound effects that are used in theater, movie, and television productions.

The sound effects are very easy to use. There are thirty-one separate categories to select from. Once you select a category, a list of all the sound effects within that category is displayed. When you select a specific sound effect, an Information window displays the file's name, and length, and a Notes window gives you a brief description of the sound clip.

My favorite sound bites are from the Speeches category. There are seven clips from John F. Kennedy, two from Douglas MacArthur, two from Richard Nixon, including his "I am not a crook" speech, and Winston Churchill's "This was their [Royal Air Force] finest hour."

InterActive Publishing has made it very easy for you to copy any of the sound files to either your hard drive, or to the Windows Clipboard for object linking and embedding in a document or presentation file. For fun you can attach any sound to a Windows system event. So when you click a button—for example YES, NO, RETRY, or HELP—a special sound will be played. There is also a CD Player and Waveform editor that can be used to edit these sound effects, or if you want, you can record your own. "1000 of the World's Greatest Sound Effects" is a must-have multimedia tool that will add new life and excitement to your documents and presentations.

"1000 of the World's Greatest Sound Effects." InterActive Publishing Corporation, 300 Airport Executive Park, Spring Valley, NY 10977; 914-426-0400. Suggested retail price: $49.95.

Would You Like a Listing of All the CD-ROMs in Print?

If you're interested in getting more information about all the CD-ROMs that are commercially available, Meckler Corporation publishes several books about CD-ROMs. Their eight-hundred-page *CD-ROMs in Print* ($76) has information on more that 3,500 CD-ROMs. It is published annually in paper and semiannually on CD-ROM. *CD-ROM Market Place* ($40) is a guide that lists the individuals who work at the different companies within the CD-ROM industry and the products that their firms make. *Business & Legal CD-ROMs in Print* ($55) is written for users and researchers in the legal and business professions. This edition lists over six hundred titles for professionals dealing with business, economics, and the law. Meckler also publishes the monthly magazine *CD-ROM World* (800-632-5537).

Meckler Corporation. 11 Ferry Lane West, Westport, CT 06880; 800-635-5537.

This Is What You Need in a CD-ROM Player

In looking for a CD-ROM player, the most important feature is the player's speed, which is measured by its access time and transfer rate. Access time refers to the amount of time it takes to locate a particular piece of information on the CD-ROM. A fast access time is important for text-based database search and retrieval applications. A very fast access time would be about 250ms (milliseconds). The data transfer rate is the amount of data that can be transferred per second from the CD-ROM to the computer once the data has been located. The industry standard is currently 150KB (Kilobytes) per second, which is fine for transferring text or sound but seems like an eternity when you're watching video clips and animation. Some of the newer CD-ROM drives have a "double speed" option. This increases the transfer of video and animation information to a rate of 300KB per second. By doubling the speed of the data transfer rate, the time lags that were associated with CD-ROM computing have been greatly reduced. This makes viewing much smoother. Future generations of CD-ROMs will have triple and quadruple speed options.

When selecting a CD-ROM player you want one that supports multiple CD-ROM platforms, including multimedia CDs, Kodak CDs, and audio CDs. Kodak's Multisession Photo-CD allows you to use your personal computer to view and manipulate 35mm images that have been transferred to a Photo-CD.

CD-ROMs are available in several different designs. There are internal units that are installed inside a personal computer, external units that sit on the desktop and are attached to the computer by a cable, and portable readers that can be attached to a laptop computer and used anywhere.

Treat Yourself to a Multimedia Package

If you're going to buy a CD-ROM, don't just buy the reader, buy an entire multimedia package. This would include a sound card, microphone, games, and software. You'll get much more value for your money. Media Vision's Pro 16 Multimedia System II bundles their award-winning Pro AudioStudio 16 sound card with NEC's top-rated MultiSpin CD-ROM drive. The package includes the most popular CD-ROM titles, including business, educational, and entertainment applications as well as the software programs that I talked about earlier: ExecuVoice, Monologue, Recording Session, and Sound Impressions. They even include a microphone.

The CD-ROM brings pictures, video, animation, and text to your computer screen, and the sound card adds music and voice as your computer comes to life. I must say that it's a real experience to click on the video clip of "bears" and watch several of them fish in a stream and listen to the noises they make in the wild. It gives me the feeling that I'm in Yellowstone Park and am watching them from the other side of the stream.

I would like to tell you a little bit about one of the CD-ROMs that comes with Media Vision's Pro 16 Multimedia System II, Compton's Interactive Encyclopedia. The multimedia package also includes some of today's most popular games: Mantis Experimental Fighter, an outer space adventure saga; Where in the World is Carmen Sandiego? the best-selling educational game that turns an exciting worldwide chase into a geography lesson; Battle Chess, a game where medieval knights, kings, queens, and pawns spring to life with amazing special effects; PC Karaoke, which allows everybody in the house to sing along to Billboard's all-time greatest hits; and Macromedia Action!, where you can create dazzling multimedia presentions that combine sound, motion, text, graphics, animation, video, and interactivity. The *Mayo Clinic Family Health Book* is also included.

I must admit that I haven't started playing the games. I know that if I did I would never have completed this book. I now look at them as my reward for this accomplishment. In the meantime let me tell you about Compton's Interactive Encyclopedia.

Pro 16 Multimedia System II. Media Vision, Inc., 47300 Bayside Parkway, Freemont, CA 94538; 800-845-5879. Suggested retail price: $1,195.

Compton's Interactive Encyclopedia

Compton's Interactive Encyclopedia for Windows contains all of the information found in the twenty-six volumes of the encyclopedia's printed version and a whole lot more. In addition to the thirty-three thousand articles—nine million words—there are ten thousand images; fifty minutes of sound, speech, and music; forty animated sequences; ninety-four videos; five thousand maps, charts, and diagrams (eight hundred of the maps are in full color); plus the complete Merriam-Webster's OnLine Dictionary.

Eleven separate paths lead you into Compton's world of information. Each path offers you a unique way of looking through the encyclopedia. Some paths group items of the same kind together, such as pictures, sounds, and videos. Others let you research an idea or topic.

Idea Search

Idea Search finds articles and pictures using a word, phrase, or question that you enter in the search request box. The computer then searches through the entire encyclopedia for those key words and

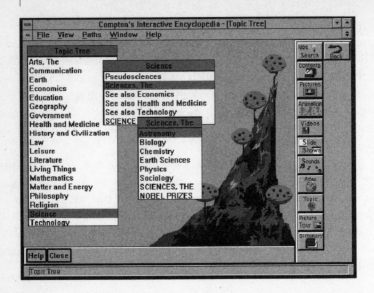

creates a list of articles or pictures that may be related to your topic. From the list you can go directly to the article or picture.

Contents

The Contents path displays an alphabetical list of every article.

Pictures

The Pictures path displays an alphabetical list of every picture. The Picture Window shows the picture together with its caption. The Picture Tour displays a selection of pictures. When you select a picture, a brief description is shown beneath it. By clicking "article," you can read a much more detailed description.

Animations

The Animations path displays a list of the animation sequences, which show and explain a process.

Videos

Videos are video clips of famous events or subjects, accompanied by a sound recording.

Sounds and Music

The Sounds path displays a list of the sounds and music in Compton's.

Slide Shows

Compton's Slide Shows consist of a series of related pictures accompanied by a sound track.

World Atlas

The World Atlas lets you explore a map of hundreds of places on the earth. Choose a place you want to see and the atlas displays the location at the center of the screen. Double click with the mouse, and Compton's shows you an article about that place.

Topic Tree

The Topic Tree organizes all the articles in Compton's into topics and subtopics. From these lists you can go directly to specific articles and begin exploring the world of Compton's. The opening screen shows an alphabetized list of nineteen topics.

Dictionary and Thesaurus

The Merriam-Webster OnLine Dictionary contains nearly seventy thousand definitions for sixty thousand words and phrases. It contains the contents of *Webster's New Ideal Dictionary, Second Edition*. The on-line thesaurus contains the complete text of *Webster's Collegiate Thesaurus*, with more than a hundred thousand synonyms, antonyms, idiomatic phrases, related words, and contrasted words. In addition, there are seven companion references and twenty tables of essential information.

A Word About Articles

As you're reading an article, different icons are displayed in the left-hand margin. These indicate that a multimedia feature—a picture, video, sound clip, or animation—is associated with the nearby text. Click on the icon and you can watch or listen to the specific multimedia feature. While reading an article, you might come across a subject or idea that you want to learn more about. You can then use the Idea Search to search through the entire encyclopedia for articles that are related to that topic. Any article within the encyclopedia can be printed. In addition you can copy any block of text from Compton's to the Windows Clipboard and then paste it in any document.

One day I stumbled onto something I found very interesting about the CD-ROM. I decided to look at the list of files on Compton's in the File Manager and saw that the files are stored in separate directories. There is a "sound" directory where the files have the *.WAV extension, an "AVI" directory for videos, and a "slide" directory for the slide shows. I clicked one of the sound files with my mouse, and lo and behold, the music began to play. Then I changed to the AVI directory, clicked on a file, and a moment later I was watching and listening to a video clip.

After a while it finally dawned on me that any of these files could be used in a multimedia presentation. All you've got to do is embed the file into your presentation using OLE. If you want you can also edit the *.WAV files in the Sound Impressions Wave Editor. With this added flexibility, you can do some wonderful things. You could also copy the *.WAV or *.AVI file from the CD-ROM and save it on your hard disk so you can play them anytime you want.

Compton's Interactive Encyclopedia is a great educational and reference tool. I must admit, when I'm wandering down Compton's different paths, I feel as if I'm in a museum and am getting my own guided tour. It's great!

Play Your Videos on Your Computer

With Media Vision's Pro MovieStudio video card you can attach your VCR, camcorder, or laser disk to your computer and add a whole new dimension to your presentations, multimedia projects, and training videos. To make your videos look their best, you can make adjustments for brightness, contrast, and individual reds, greens, and blues. While watching digital movies, you can click and freeze individual frames, which enables you to easily store single images for use in your other applications.

Pro MovieStudio. Media Vision, Inc., 47300 Bayside Parkway, Freemont, CA 94538; 800-845-5879. Suggested retail price: $449.

Part III

WINNING THE FIGHT BETWEEN
YOU AND YOUR COMPUTER

Organize Your Hard Drive

Nobody ever has enough space on their hard drives. And until you actually get rid of old files and unused programs, you don't realize how much space is being wasted. We all make it a point, or at least we should, to clean out our office filing cabinets regularly, and a hard drive is just an electronic filing cabinet. And like traditional filing cabinets, if you continue to add more and more files without deleting old and unused files, the cabinet will eventually become stuffed beyond capacity, making it impossible to find the papers or documents you need.

Delete or Move Old Files

Delete Backup Files

The first step in organizing the files on your hard drive should be deleting all your old or unnecessary files. The easiest place to start is with your backup files. Many programs have a feature that automatically backs up a file. You can recognize a backup file because it has the extension *.BK! or *.BAK. The backup program works like this. You create a file that we'll call C:\LETTER. A little while later you decide to make a change to this document, so you open the file, make your changes, and then save it. With the automatic backup program, the original version of C:\LETTER becomes C:\LETTER.BAK and the revised version is now C:\LETTER. You can always see which version of a file is older by looking at the date and time it was last saved. If you've been using the automatic backup system, you may have a backup file for every one of your files. These backup files are certainly taking up valuable space on your hard drive.

It's very easy to get rid of your backup files. First you open your File Manager and select a directory. All the files within the directory will be displayed. Then you do a search for all the files with the *.BAK extension. Once the search is completed, which only takes a second, all the files with the *.BAK extension will be displayed. You can delete the files one at a time, or by holding down the SHIFT key while clicking your mouse, you can select a group of files and delete them at once.

Delete Unneeded Files

Now that you've gotten rid of your backup files, you should delete old files that you no longer need. I'm sure you've got plenty of them. You can do this in one of two ways—with the File Manager or from within the program that created the file.

Select a directory and browse through the files, one at a time. If you no longer need a file, delete it. If you're not sure at this particular moment whether or not it should be kept, create an archive directory where you can store these old files. This step gets them out of the way. In the future you can go in and delete the ones you no longer need.

Keeping Permanent Files

Finally, you've got files that you do wish to keep but won't need to look at very often. If you want to keep these files on your hard drive, create a permanent archive directory where you can move them just to get them out of the way. If you don't want them on your hard drive, copy them to a floppy disk that you can either store in a desk drawer or in the hard copy file that has additional information relating to the information on the disk.

When you save files on a disk, be sure to give it a label that describes the files and print a hard copy of the disk's directories and subdirectories. You may also want to write additional notes as to the nature of the files. Fold the paper until it's the same size as the disk and use a rubber band to keep it securely attached. Now you'll always know what files are on the disk—even if you don't look at it for a year.

Dealing with Someone Else's Old Files

In the old days, when everybody had papers and nobody used computers, a person would move into a new office and inherit the files of the previous occupant. These files usually remained in a file drawer untouched and unused. This is one reason why so many people have piles of papers on their desk. The file cabinets are filled with old papers that are never looked at again.

Today when a person begins working at a new desk, they inherit the previous occupant's computer: files and all. In most cases, the person hasn't got the slightest idea as to what these files are or why they're there. If this has happened to you, here are some things you should do. Open the directory where the files are stored and:

- Check the dates of the files to determine how old they are. In the File Manager you can sort the files by date, with the newest file positioned at the top of the list. (Make sure you're looking at data files, not program or system files.) You'll quickly see that some of the files are so old there can't possibly be any reason to keep them.
- View the files to determine if there is anything that may be important or meaningful. If there is, either: (1) print it out, file the hard copy away, and delete the file, or (2) should it be preferable to keep the file stored on the hard drive, move it to one of the directories you've created. Don't leave it in the old directory. Finally, if the file isn't important, delete it.
- If you want to keep some or all of the files, just to be sure that you don't get rid of something important, you've two choices. You can leave them alone for the time being and make a note that sometime in the future the files should be purged, or you can save the files to a floppy disk and put it away in a desk drawer.

Do You Have Hard Copies of Your Computer Files?

If you've got hard copies of your computer files, do you need to keep both the hard copy *and* the computer file? Many people like to store all the documents and other pertinent information they have about a particular person, client, or project in the same file folder. This way everything is easy to locate.

Delete Unused Programs

Once you've disposed of your old document files, you have got the problem of disposing of your old program files. We've all got programs that we no longer use. Maybe you still have the DOS version of a program, even though you've been using the Windows version for a year. Or you replaced one program with a better one, but never got rid of the old one. And we've all installed software that we tried for a few days or weeks, found we didn't like, and never used again. But for some strange reason we never got around to removing it from the hard drive. In addition, we've got parts of applications, like the tutorial that came with the word processor, that are taking up space and should be deleted.

Deleting a DOS program is easy because all you've got to do is open the File Manager, go to the directory that contains the program's files, mark the files, and press the DELETE key. But getting rid of a Windows program is more complicated. Deleting the icon that's displayed in the Program Manager doesn't delete the files that run the program, it just deletes the symbol that turns the program on. And if you delete the program files in the same way you deleted DOS files, there may still be some program instructions remaining.

In Windows, there are specific files that make the operating environment work. These files are called *initialization* files, and have the "*.INI" extension. Every Windows application has its own "*.INI" file. In the Windows directory, there is a master file, "WIN.INI," which has additional information about every program you've installed. These "*.INI" files provide Windows with the specific setup and operating instructions of each program so it can run properly.

When you first install Windows, the list of instructions in the WIN.INI file is relatively short because you haven't installed many Windows programs. But every time you install a new Windows application, the application adds its specific instructions to the WIN.INI file. The more applications you have, the larger the WIN.INI file becomes.

"Uninstall" Your Windows Programs

Now trying to delete specific lines from the WIN.INI file can be rather tricky and complicated, especially if you're not an experienced computer user. So instead of trying to delete all these program files, icons, and lines of *.INI text yourself—and possibly delete something that you shouldn't—there's an easy-to-use utility program, UnInstaller, that will do it for you.

When you run UnInstaller, it first deletes the application's files from its directory and subdirectories, deletes those directories from the hard drive, removes the icon from the program group, and the program group from the Program Manager.

Then UnInstaller searches the Windows directory for the WIN.INI file and, once found, goes into the file to look for any instructions that pertain to the application that you are removing. When these instructions are found, they are also removed. When UnInstaller is finished, *all* the references to the deleted program have been removed from your computer.

Running UnInstaller is easy. You select the DOS or Windows program you want to delete from a list of all the installed programs on your computer. Then the program is "analyzed" and a list of "items to be deleted" is created. You review this list of suggested deletions and can accept or modify the list.

Once you begin the actual uninstall process, you'll be prompted before each group of files is deleted. If you approve of the deletions, you click the OK button, and the group of files is gone. The whole process can be completed in just a few minutes. When it's all done, an itemized report can be printed listing the details of the applications and files that were deleted. This way you have a written record of what was deleted.

UnInstaller works on both networks and stand-alone computers. When the network administrator uninstalls a program, UnInstaller leaves a decoy, a copy of itself on the server, in place of the original program. As other network users try to run the uninstalled application, UnInstaller offers to remove references to the application from their systems as well.

UnInstaller. MicroHelp, Inc., 439 Shallowford Industrial Parkway, Marietta, GA 30066; 800-922-3383. Suggested retail price: $79.

Double the Capacity of Your Hard Drive

Now that you've cleaned up your hard drive, how would you like to double its storage capacity? Nobody ever has enough disk space, but one way to have more is by using a data compression program.

A data compression program doesn't actually make your drive twice as big; it makes your files half as large. To compress a file, the data compression program searches for repetitive strings of characters. When a match is found, a token is inserted as a replacement.

I would like to use the sentence *Now is the time for all good men to come to the aid of their country* as an example of how data compression works. This sentence contains sixty-nine characters, including spaces. By studying it you will see that there are several character patterns that repeat themselves. The pattern __the with a space in front of *the* appears three times, and the following patterns each appear twice: __to__ with a space before and after; __co with a space before; and the pattern *me*. We can compress the amount of space needed to type the sentence by assigning a single character to represent these patterns. A "+" represents __the, "#" represents __to__, "&" represents *co*, and "@" represents *me*. With these tokens inserted for their assigned characters, the sentence now looks like this: *Now is + time for all good @n#&@#+ aid of +ir &untry.*

By substituting single characters for the repetitive letters and space patterns, the eighteen characters in the phrase *men to come to the* has been compressed to seven characters: *@n#&@#+*. Overall, I've been able to reduce the number of characters in the sentence from sixty-nine to fifty-one. That's a 26 percent reduction—a compression ratio of 1.35 to 1.

The process that I have just described is done by the computer using complex mathematical algorithms. With these calculations, the computer's capable of compressing and decompressing system files, program files, and data files in a fraction of a second. It all happens so quickly that you aren't even aware of it. As a general rule, word processing files tend to compress to half their original size, while database and spreadsheet files compress even more. Program and command files tend to compress less because they don't contain much repetitive data.

After compressing your disk drive, you still use your computer just as you did before. When you open a file, the data is decompressed and expands back to its original size for use within your program. When the file is saved, it's automatically compressed to save space. The beauty of a data compression program is that it's transparent. Once installed, it stays in the background. You never even know it's there. The only thing you will notice is that you can store twice as much data on your hard disk.

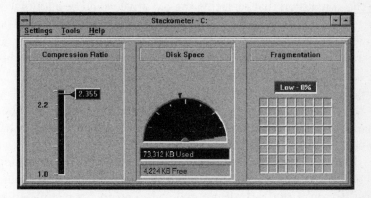

Stac Electronics, 5993 Avenida Encinas, Carlsbad, CA 92008, 800-522-7822, makes a product called **Stacker** that is easy to install and use, regardless of how your system is set up. It is designed to work with both MS-DOS 5.0 and in place of MS-DOS 6.0's Double Space. Suggested retail price: $139.95.

MS-DOS 6.0. Microsoft Corporation, One Microsoft Way, Redmond, WA 98052; 206-882-8080. Microsoft has added a data compression feature, Double Space, in its most recent version of its disk operating system MS-DOS 6.0.

Add a Second Disk Drive If You Still Need More Disk Space

Cleaning up your hard drive and installing a data compression program will buy you some time, but eventually your hard drive is going to run out of space. There are so many new productivity-improving programs that have just come on the market that you're making a big mistake if you don't get some of them for yourself. The big question is, Where do you put them? The answer is an easy one: Add a second drive.

I recently did that myself. My old 40MB drive, which had become an 80MB drive as a result of the magic of Stacker, had run out of space. When this happened I discussed my problem with some friends who knew more about computers than I did and quickly came to the conclusion that replacing the old drive would be a lot of work, since I wanted to keep all of my old programs and data files. I would have to back up my old drive, 75MB of data, onto floppy disks, and then reinstall the information on my new drive once it had been installed inside my computer. As an alternative, they suggested I do something else: Add a second disk drive.

So I went out and bought a 245MB drive from Maxtor Corporation. This way I could leave my first drive alone and wouldn't have to back up any data at all.

If you're comfortable working inside your computer, installing a second drive isn't very difficult and should take about an hour at most. If you're not technically inclined, a computer technician can come out and install the new drive for you. A few quick words of advice however: Don't start this project on a weekend or after-hours. If you run into some technical problems, have some questions, or find yourself getting into trouble, you won't be able to call technical assistance for any help or advice.

In addition, there is some basic information you will need before you or the technician begins to install the new drive. You need to know the name of the manufacturer and the model number of your original hard drive so you can contact them and get the correct settings for the drive's jumper switches. (A jumper switch is a series of three pins with a sleeve that slides over two of them. Depending upon the desired setting, the sleeve will connect pins 1 and 2, 2 and 3, or none at all.)

A hard drive can be configured in one of three ways: As a single drive, a "master" drive on a two-drive system, or as a "slave" drive on a two-drive system. (I know these are terrible names! But that is what they're *actually* called.) The jumper settings tell the computer how many drives you have. If you've got two drives, it tells the computer which drive is the slave and which is the master. You set your original drive as the master drive and set the second drive as the slave. Your life will be much easier if you've got this information for both your drives before you start working on your computer.

You will also need to know the configuration settings for both of your drives. (The settings for the new drive should be included in the installation manual.) You need this information because once you've installed the drives, you must tell the computer the size and type of hard drives that are on your system. When you call the manufacturer of your original disk drive, they can give you this information at the same time they give you the jumper settings. You can also get this information by running the "setup" program in your computer.

When you turn on your computer, push the DELETE key. You'll go into the CMOS setup, and when you open the "STANDARD CMOS SETUP" directory, you'll see the settings for your hard drive. They will be displayed in a format that looks like: Type-17, Cyln-977, Head-5, WPcom-300, LZone-977, Sect-17, Size-41MB. Write down these settings and exit out of the CMOS setup. Don't make any changes to your system. I also don't know what all these numbers or categories mean either, but when you restart your computer after installing the new drives, you'll have to reenter this information into the CMOS setup for both the master and slave drives before your computer will run again. Your master drive will be drive "C" and your slave drive will be drive "D."

Maxtor Corporation makes a complete line of hard disk drives. Maxtor Corporation, 2190 Miller Drive, Longmont, CO 80501; 800-262-9867.

Set up a Usable Filing System

One of the biggest problems everybody has in working within the DOS operating environment comes from the system's inability to accept file names that mean something. With DOS you're limited to an eight-character file name with a three-character extension. Since my expertise is in file and paper management and my specialty is in helping people organize their desks and filing cabinets, I've certainly got some ideas on how a disk drive should be organized.

From my perspective, a disk drive is nothing more than an electronic filing cabinet. I would like to tell you about some of the things I've seen that you shouldn't do. If you were to set up an office filing system, would you throw all your paper in the drawers of a filing cabinet without organizing them first? Well, people do it with their computer files. I know one person who had a 200MB hard drive and installed a data compression program to expand it to 400MBs. Now he has so many files in so few directories that he loses track of everything. In his root directory [C:\] alone he has 388 files. If you don't organize your computer files, you'll eventually be working in chaos.

Another mistake people often make is storing their document files in the same directory as their operating system or program files. If you store files in this manner, you're flirting with disaster, because it's too easy to accidentally delete a program or system file, thinking it was an old letter or memo you no longer needed. Do this, and you'll quickly discover that your word processor or even your computer won't run—and you won't have the slightest idea why.

And don't make your root directory, [C:\], your default directory. The default directory is the directory in which every file is automatically saved. Your root directory should be reserved for your program and working file directories and the handful of files that are needed to make your computer run, like the CONFIG.SYS and AUTOEXEC.BAT files.

Another way people try to distinguish among files is by using the three-character extension, such as *.DOC for documents, *.PRO for proposals, *.MEM for memo, etc. I think it makes much more sense to set up separate directories and subdirectories that can be used to store similar types of information. When you set up your directories in a logical, systematic manner, you'll save yourself hours of time in the future.

For example, if you've got a big client who generates a lot of correspondence, set up a separate directory for this person or firm and don't mix these files with any other files. Give the directory a name

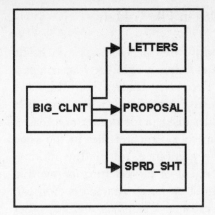
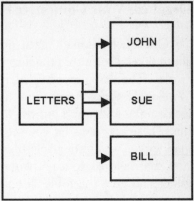

like BIG__CLNT. Now you'll probably have different kinds of files for this client, so you should have separate directories named: LET-TERS, PROPOSAL, SPRD__SHT, or any other topic or category that you feel would be appropriate. And when you give these files a name, pick one that means something to you. Don't name your files by the date created. How will you know what's in a file with a name like: C:\LETTERS\01-07.DOC? Wouldn't it make more sense to give it a name like C:\LETTERS\SALESCON, for a document that was written concerning a sales contract. Or if you have different versions of the contract, start numbering them by using the three-character extension: SALESCON.1, SALESCON.2. With this method of organizing and naming your directories and files, you'll be able to locate your files in a matter of moments.

If you send correspondence to several people regularly, why not create separate subsubdirectories to store their correspondence. As shown in the illustration, if you regularly send letters to John, Sue, and Bill, create separate subdirectories under the LETTERS subdirectory. This way you can keep all your correspondence organized.

For myself, I'm constantly creating new directories and subdirectories as I try to group similar topics and subjects together. When a directory begins to get too large—more than fifty files—I begin to look for files that relate to one another or that can be grouped together. Then I move them into a new subdirectory. This way I've found that it's easy to manage my files.

Organize Your Computer Files in File Folders

One day I was reading the morning newspaper and saw an article about several software programs that help you organize your computer files. The designers of Golden Retriever; Ready, Aim, FILE!; and Windows Express have come up with a novel idea. Put your files inside a file folder and put the folder inside a file drawer or a master file. These programs let you set up your computer files in the same manner you set up the paper files in your office. You put the information that belongs to a particular client or project into its own file folder and give the folder a name of up to 16 characters. You can group your letters, documents, spreadsheets, graphics, and any other files you may have in the same file folder, which can have a name of up to 256 characters, without any concern or regard to which DOS directory they happen to be physically stored in or which computer application you used to create them. This gives you the opportunity to see everything you have on a specific subject, client, prospect, or job at once—in the same file folder. Click on the item in the file folder and the program that works with the file is launched, and the file itself is opened.

When you create an entry for a new file, you can also include a document summary that has information about the subject, author,

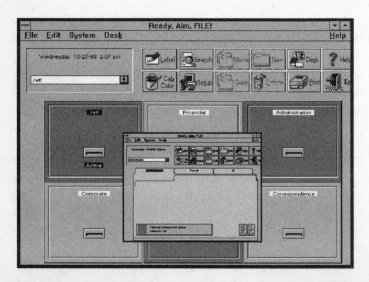

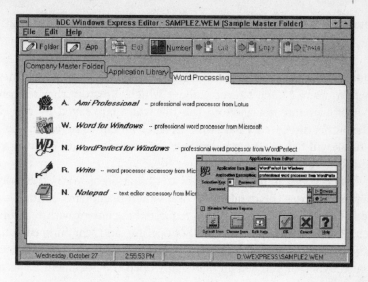

recipient, status, and a free form field where you can include additional comments.

Golden Retriever; Ready, Aim, FILE!; and Windows Express all offer a great alternative to DOS's limited file management capabilities. With an easy-to-use filing system, you'll find yourself saving hours of time when you're looking for that one document that's stored among thousands.

Golden Retriever: Above Software, Inc., 2698 White Road, Suite 200, Irvine, CA 92714; 800-344-0116. Suggested retail price: $99.00

Ready, Aim, FILE! V Soft Development Corporation, 346 State Place, Escondido, CA 92029; 800-845-4843. Suggested retail price: $129.95

Windows Express. HDC Computer Corporation, 6742 185th Avenue NE, Redmond, WA 98052; 800-321-4606. Suggested retail price: $99.95.

Turn Your Computer into a Personal Research Assistant, Filing Clerk, and Paper Chaser

Another possible solution for locating your files is by indexing them. Then you don't have to worry about which directory they're stored in or what name you gave to the file when you saved it. You can index a file, directory, a hard disk drive, or an entire network, and by doing so will have created a database that contains a list of every key word that was used in every indexed file.

When you search for a word, or combination of words, the indexing program uses the database to find which documents contain that word. This allows you to locate a requested document within seconds because it scans the index instead of opening and searching each file. You can then view the documents you want with the built-in document browser, or you can automatically open the document using the application that created it.

So when you want to find that letter you sent to John Jones, you search for "John Jones," and a list of every file that contains "John Jones" is displayed. If the search retrieves more files than you can easily work with, you can initiate a second search from within this

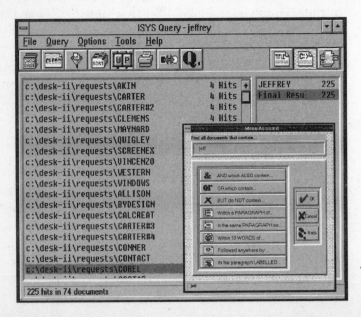

list, this one for "new business proposal," and the list of files that contain these words will be displayed. When the desired file is located, you can launch the program that created the file, and that file will be automatically opened. All of the popular word processing, database, and text formats are supported.

With an indexing program you'll always be able to locate any letter, document, or spreadsheet in just a few seconds. And you will never have to waste valuable time searching through files, directories, hard drives, or even the network server. Both Eclipse FIND and ISYS are available for the stand-alone and network users.

Eclipse Find. Phoenix Technologies Ltd., 846 University Avenue, Norwood, MA 06062; 800-278-7197. Suggested retail price: $89.95.

ISYS. Odyssey Development, Inc., 650 South Cherry Street, Denver, CO 80222; 800-992-4797. Suggested retail price for the single user: $395; for three-station concurrent user: $795; five-station concurrent user: $1,295.

Back up Your Work

One of the things you should *always* do is back up your work. You may feel that it isn't necessary because you've got a good, dependable computer system, but, in reality, you're making a big mistake. Sooner or later everybody has some sort of computer failure. You may just lose the data that was on the screen when the computer died; there could be some sort of mechanical failure where data on the hard drive is lost (I'll discuss on page 192 how you can recover lost data); or your computer could become infected with a virus. If you haven't made it a point to regularly back up your work, it may take you hours, days, or it may not even be possible to restore everything. It's an absolute nightmare to discover that several important files have disappeared—and there's no way to get them back.

When you think about backing up your work, there are several areas of concern: (1) losing the information that's on the screen if the computer suddenly has some sort of failure; and (2) losing important data or information before you could perform your regular back-up.

Automatic Backup Features

Most programs have a feature that will automatically back up the file that you're currently working on while you actually have the document on the screen. In the event your computer locks up and you're forced to restart your computer or the program abruptly stops running and you suddenly find yourself at a C prompt [C:\]—both have happened to me on far more occasions than I will admit to—and you're not using the automatic backup feature, all the changes you made to your document since it was opened will be lost. You may lose just five minutes, or several hours, of work. In either case, you'll have to start from scratch.

With the automatic backup the program will save a copy of your file at regular intervals, such as every fifteen minutes, and should you have a failure, you'll only lose the information that had changed between the time of the last backup and the time of the failure. When you restart the program, you'll be informed that a backup file exists and asked if you want to save it. Answer "yes," give it a new file name, and you've just saved yourself hours of additional work.

I can't tell you how many times I've had to reboot my machine because it had locked up and, as a result, lost a great deal of work. As a writer, it isn't easy reconstructing the sentences and phrases I had written just fifteen minutes earlier.

Today I've got my automatic backup set at five minutes. If I have a failure, I will only lose data that was five minutes old. In addition, I make it a point to always save my file to my hard drive at regular intervals, especially if I'm about to take a phone call or when someone walks into the room to ask a question or start a conversation. The last thing I want to happen is to lose information because I was careless.

Copy Important Files to a Floppy Disk

Now you may think I'm being paranoid about losing a file, but I've learned from experience that when I'm working on something important, like this book for instance, I will not only save the file to my hard drive, I'll make a copy of it on a floppy disk. This way I'm protected should something happen to my hard drive and damage my files before I run my regularly scheduled backup program. Even if, God forbid, my hard drive is wiped out, I've still got the floppy disk. (I'll talk about dealing with a disk drive failure a little later.)

Install a Hard Disk Backup Program

Automatic backups are a great program feature, and you should make it a habit of copying selected files to a floppy disk. Unfortunately, these steps are only a partial solution to the much larger problem of protecting your data. What would you do if you had some sort of hard disk failure and not only lost files that had important information but also lost the files that make your programs run—such as your word

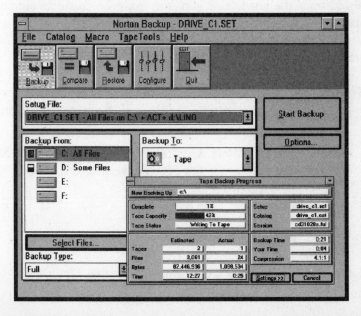

processor, spreadsheet, database, or personal information manager, and even your system—DOS and Windows—files that make your computer work.

Now you've got a BIG!!! problem. The easiest way to insure that this never happens to you is to install an automated backup program like Norton Backup or Central Point Software's PC Tools. These programs are both fast, easy to use, and can be real lifesavers in the event of a disaster.

When you back up your hard drive, you're making a complete copy of all your files—system files, application files, and data files—onto floppy disks or a tape drive. Should you have a computer failure and files are damaged, you can then restore the information to your computer from your backup disks.

It's recommended that you do a complete backup of your hard drive once a week, perhaps every Friday afternoon. Your backup disks should be stored in a safe place, preferably an inexpensive fireproof safe. Because you're using your computer every day, you're going to be creating new files and making changes to others. However, you don't need to back up your entire disk drive just because a handful of files have changed. Instead, you back up only the files that have changed since the last full backup. You can even create an automated backup schedule where the program will run every afternoon at four-thirty. With this kind of backup program, your data will be fully protected should the unthinkable happen.

Norton Backup. Symantec Corporation, 10201 Torre Avenue, Cupertino, CA 95014; 800-441-7234. Suggested retail price: $149.

Central Point PC Tools. Central Point Software, 15220 NW Greenbrier Parkway, Suite 200, Beaverton, OR 97006; 800-365-8090. Suggested retail price: $179.

Use a Tape Drive

There's only one problem with using floppy disks to back up your data: They don't hold enough information. Even with data compression, a 1.44MB floppy disk can't hold much more than 2.5MB of data. This was fine when programs were small and most computers had 40MB hard drives. You only needed twelve to fifteen floppy disks to do a full backup, and the whole process took ten to fifteen minutes.

Today's computers have hard drives that are considerably larger. Even a 100MB drive now seems small. On my computer I've got two disk drives. My original 40MB drive has doubled to 80MB through the use of a Stacker. My second drive is 245MB. At the moment, I've got more than 200MB of data stored inside my computer. If I were to try to back up my computer with floppy disks, I would need at least eighty disks. It would take more than an hour. To solve this problem, I bought a 250MB Jumbo Tape Drive from Colorado Memory Systems, Inc.

With the tape drive, the whole process of backing up my drive has been automated. I no longer have to sit by the machine and insert empty disks into "drive A" every few minutes as they reach their storage capacity. I just insert the tape, turn on the backup program, and with Window's ability to run programs in the background, I can go back to work at the same time my disk drive is being backed up. I've even set up my daily backup schedule so that the program runs every afternoon at 5:00 P.M. I don't even have to be present. My only responsibility is to make sure there's a tape in the drive. Another advantage of using a tape drive is that it's fast. You can back up your data at 6MB to 8MB a minute.

I believe that everybody should have a tape drive installed in their computer. Without one, you'll probably never get around to backing up your hard drive because using floppy disks is too much work.

A tape drive is easy to install. If you have an open bay, an internal tape drive can be installed inside your computer. Or you can use a cable to attach an external backup to one of your computer's serial ports. Either way, a tape drive makes backing up your data a breeze.

Jumbo Tape Backup System. Colorado Memory Systems, Inc., 800 S. Taft Avenue, Loveland, CO 80537; 800-451-4523. Colorado Memory Systems makes many different sizes and types of tape drives.

If Your Computer Won't Start, Restart It with a Bootable Floppy

Occasionally something happens that causes your computer to lock up, and for some unknown reason, it's impossible to restart your computer. I'm not going even to try to give you the reasons why this could happen. Take my word for it, it does—and if you can't get the system up and running, it's almost impossible to solve the problem that caused it to shut down. For this reason, you should always keep a formatted system disk available.

A system disk, sometimes called a *bootable floppy*, is a floppy disk that contains only the files required to start your system. When you start your computer with a floppy disk in "drive A," the computer is using those files to start the computer, not the files that are on your hard drive, which are the ones that are causing the problem.

To create a system disk exit to a DOS prompt:

- Change to the DOS directory, by typing CD C:\DOS. (CD stands for change directory.)
- Insert a formatted blank disk into drive A.
- Type SYS A:

This will copy the necessary system files to the floppy disk. If you're in Windows, you can also format a system disk from the File Manager. Select DISK from the pull-down menu, and then select MAKE SYSTEM DISK. If you're using a data compression program, like Stacker, you need to copy your CONFIG.SYS file, which is found in your root [C:\] directory, onto the floppy disk. The one line that must be present is the one that loads Stacker, C:\STACKER\STACKER.COM. Without the STACKER.COM line, it's impossible to open the compressed drive, which has all of your files on it. Your system disk should be properly labeled and stored in a safe place.

Make a Copy of Your Computer's Configuration Files

There are a number of files that have been created to tell your computer what programs you've installed and how you want your system to operate. These are your CONFIG.SYS, AUTOEXEC.BAT, found in your root [C:\] directory, and WINDOWS.INI and SYSTEM.INI files, which are found in your Windows directory. And there are configuration settings that tell the computer what type of hardware is installed, such as the type of monitor you have, and the configuration settings of your hard drive.

If you were to have a failure and these files were to become damaged or the configuration settings had to be reinstalled on the computer, it could take you a lot of time to try and reconstruct this information. An easy way to protect yourself is to make a hard copy of all the computer's files and settings and put it with your computer manuals.

As part of the Windows operating system there is a program called Microsoft Diagnostics that tells you the status of every setting inside your computer. To open Microsoft Diagnostics, go to a DOS prompt [C:\]—you must exit Windows first—and type MSD. If nothing happens, change to the Windows directory by typing CD C:\WIN-

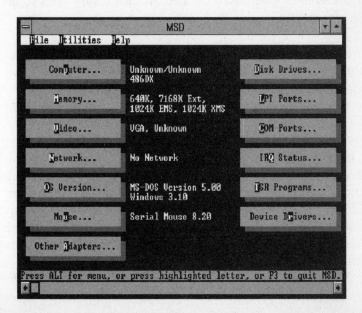

DOWS, and press ENTER. Then type MSD. The diagnostics program will open in a few moments. You can copy the entire program by selecting FILE from the pull-down menu and then PRINT.

This printed report will give you the complete status of your entire computer system, including information about the system's memory, video card, operating system, mouse, disk drives (including the settings for the configuration of your hard drives, which is very important), LPT and COM ports, IRQ status, a complete list of any terminate and stay resident programs (TSRs) and device drivers you're running, and complete copies of your AUTOEXEC.BAT, CONFIG.SYS, SYSTEM.INI, and WIN.INI files.

I'm sure that you won't have the slightest idea what most of this information means, and, to tell you the truth, neither do I. But in the event that you do have some sort of computer problem, the access to this information can save you hours of time in trying to reconstruct your system. This report should be put away in a file or with your computer manuals.

Recover Your Data if the Unthinkable Happens: Your Hard Drive Is Damaged or You Accidentally Delete an Important File

In the event you do have an emergency and have lost files, Norton Utilities has several utility programs that will help you restore your hard disk and recover damaged or accidentally deleted files. In this case, the first thing you should do is nothing. Any new files copied to your hard disk might overwrite existing data, preventing you from recovering your damaged or deleted files.

If you have previously installed Norton Utilities, you can use it to restore your lost or damaged data. If you purchase Norton Utilities after a disaster has occurred, *do not install* the utilities program on your hard drive because you could overwrite some of your data. You can recover your data by using the Utilities Emergency Disk, which comes with the program. You insert the Emergency Disk—which has all the necessary files you need to recover your data—in your floppy disk drive, and then go through the process, step-by-step, of recovering your damaged data. Norton Utilities can restore damaged Lotus 1-2-3, Symphony, Excel, Quatro Pro, dBase, and WordPerfect files.

Norton Utilities. Symantec Corporation, 10201 Torre Avenue, Cupertino, CA 95014; 800-441-7234. Suggested retail price: $179.

Protect Your Computer from Viruses

A *computer virus* is an infectious computer program that places copies of itself into other application and program files, disrupting the normal activities of these files once the program is run. Though many viruses are destructive, some are merely annoying, doing little damage other than replicating themselves and displaying cute messages. But the worst type of virus incorporates a *logic bomb*—a destructive code that waits until a particular date arrives or another condition is met to permanently destroy files or even erase the entire contents of your computer by reformatting your hard disk. Some viruses wait quietly for the logic bomb trigger date—and then explode without warning. Others announce themselves through obvious symptoms, like flashing a message across your screen.

Though everybody who uses a computer is potentially at risk, there are some activities that greatly increase the probability that you will infect your computer with a virus. If you do any of the following you're putting your computer in the high-risk category:

- Do you ever download programs from private bulletin board services?
- Do you ever copy files from other systems using floppy disks?
- Are you hooked up to a LAN?

What Does a Virus Do?

When discussing viruses, two terms are commonly used: Trojan horse, and worm. A Trojan horse is a program that appears to serve some useful purpose, which encourages you to run it. But like the Trojan horse of old, it has a covert purpose. Once inside your computer, it wants to disrupt your system and damage your files. A worm is a virus that duplicates itself, creating myriad copies all running simultaneously, to slow down your computer. Some worms spread by copying their own program files from disk to disk, while others replicate themselves only in memory.

There are several types of viruses that can attack your computer.

Program Infecting Viruses

This type of virus attacks executable program files. Some viruses replace a portion of the original program files' code with their own, thus damaging the files irreparably. Others add themselves to program files in a way that allows the original programs still to function. Once an infected program is executed, a program infector will remain active in your computer's memory until you turn off or restart your computer. While active, the virus continues to infect other programs and can interfere with the normal operation of your computer. Many of these types of viruses can be removed from infected files with an antivirus program, restoring them to healthy condition.

Boot-Sector/Partition-Table Viruses

These viruses substitute themselves for either one or both of two special programs used by your computer when you turn on, or reboot, it. The computer first verifies its memory and performs other hardware checks, then it determines which disk it will attempt to load DOS from. To do this it looks for the master-boot program that is located on your hard disk in the partition-table sector. Once the master-boot program takes over, it loads something called "the boot sector program," which continues the process of booting your computer.

A partition-table virus substitutes itself for the master-boot program, while a boot-sector virus substitutes itself for the boot-sector program. Therefore, this type of virus causes the most injury and damage to a computer system because it becomes active each time the computer starts. The only way to remove this virus is by starting the computer with a virus-free floppy disk and then removing it from either the partition-table or the boot-sector of your hard disk.

These two special sectors are located outside of the area of the disk where program and system files are stored, which makes it impossible to remove a boot-sector or a partition-table virus by deleting or replacing files. These viruses can only be removed by an antivirus program like Norton AntiVirus.

Prevention Is Your Best Protection

To keep your system free of viruses, there are a handful of things you should do:

- Back up your files regularly. Do a full backup once a week with daily incremental backups. If your computer is infected with a virus, you must remember to disinfect the restored files.
- Don't boot your computer with a floppy disk that you haven't scanned and disinfected first.
- It is through the importation of files from other computers that you run the greatest risk of infecting your own computer. Copying files from a floppy diskette is one of the most common ways for a virus to spread. Make it a point to scan every program you download from a bulletin board service (BBS) or copy from a floppy disk or network drive, before running them on your computer.
- Install an antivirus program and use the memory-resident virus-spotting portion of the program at all times. If you suspect that your computer has an infection, turn off your computer immediately, reboot from a clean floppy (one without an AUTOEXEC.BAT or a CONFIG.SYS file), and then disinfect the system, using a disk-based copy of your antivirus program.

Norton AntiVirus scans your files and your directories whenever your computer is turned on. It can also scan each floppy disk for viruses before files are copied onto your computer. Should a virus be detected, Norton AntiVirus can quickly repair infected files.

Norton Antivirus. Symantec Corporation, 10201 Torre Avenue, Cupertino, CA 95014; 800-441-7234. Suggested retail price: $129.

Improve the Performance of Your Computer and Your Software

You'll Never Be "Out of Memory" When You Use a Memory Manager

Have you ever had an "out of memory" message flash on your screen as you tried to use one of your program's advanced features or found that for some unknown reason you were unable to load a program into memory? If this happens frequently, it's a good indication that your computer's memory isn't being properly allocated. With a memory manager, you can greatly increase the amount of memory that's available to run your favorite programs.

Regardless of how much memory your computer has, it's the first megabyte, 1048K, of memory that's used to run your computer. Conventional memory takes up the first 640K. High memory takes up the balance, 384K. It is in the first 640K that DOS, your device drivers, your mouse, your scanner, your modem, and any terminate and stay resident programs (TSRs)—like your fax program, your dictionary/thesaurus program, and all of your operating programs, such

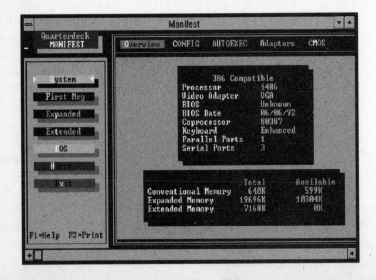

as your word processor, spreadsheet—are loaded. The software that controls such system functions as the display monitor, keyboard, and printer are loaded into high memory. If too many things are loaded into conventional memory, there may not be enough room remaining to load a software or spreadsheet program.

To help you visualize how conventional and upper memory works, imagine an empty street. On both sides of the street there are street addresses, but no buildings. No houses. No offices. No stores. Each lot is vacant. That's what your computer's memory looks like when the machine is off. But once you turn it on, there's a mad rush by the DOS operating system, the monitor, keyboard, printer, mouse, backup tape drive, scanner, fax modem, CD-ROM, and anything else you've installed on your computer to claim an address on the street and put up a building.

There is no zoning, so each land grabber takes a few addresses without any regard to saving some additional space for another user. If a few vacant lots too small to build on are squeezed between some buildings, those addresses can't be used. On the conventional memory side of the street there are 640,000 addresses. Whatever addresses are still vacant after you've turned on your computer are available for your programs, like your word processor or spreadsheet.

Across the street, on the upper memory block, there are 384,000 addresses. These addresses are taken by the parts of the computer's operating system that control such pieces of hardware as the display monitor, keyboard, and printer. Though there are 384,000 addresses, these pieces of hardware only use a portion of it.

A memory manager acts like the local zoning board. It moves some of the programs, including the DOS operating system, device drivers, and TSRs that had previously been loaded into conventional memory into the unused addresses in upper memory, making sure that no block of upper memory remains vacant. Since these applications were moved, you've now got more room in which to run your word processor, spreadsheet, or database programs.

I installed a memory manager, QEMM-386, on my computer and found it made much more memory available. Before I ran QEMM's configuration program, I had 543.1K of available conventional memory. Afterward this increased to 618.9K, an increase of 13 percent. To say it another way, before QEMM I was utilizing 84 percent of my computer's memory. Now I'm using 96 percent.

> **QEMM-386.** Quarterdeck Office Systems, 150 Pico Boulevard, Santa Monica, CA 90405; 800-354-3222. Suggested retail price: $99.95

> **DOS 6.0** includes a memory management feature called MemMaker. Microsoft Corporation, One Microsoft Way, Redmond, WA 98052; 800-426-9400. Suggested retail price: $129.95.

Make Your Computer Run Faster with Disk Caching

Along with the two problems of a lack of storage space on the hard drive and in the working memory, most people experience a third problem: The system is never fast enough. Reading information off a disk drive is a mechanical process that takes time—usually 15 milliseconds—and is one of the slowest parts of a computer system.

A disk cache (pronounced CASH) makes a computer run faster and speeds up application response time because it is able to access

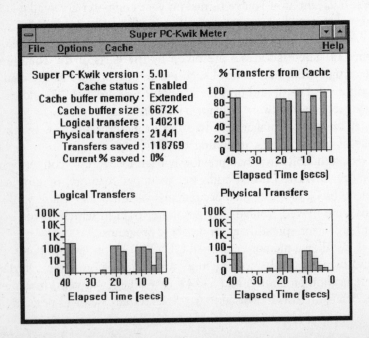

information electronically—about .012 milliseconds. A disk cache copies frequently used program data into random access memory (RAM) and reads more data into RAM than the application has actually requested. When the information is needed, it's accessed electronically, and your computer's performance improves because the disk cache reduces the number of times your application needs to access data from a hard disk.

Super PC-KWIK. PC-KWIK offers a disk caching program, Super PC-KWIK, and a companion product, PC-KWIK Power Pack, which has utilities that make your screen scroll faster, speed up your keyboard, and give you more control over your printing. PC-Kwik Corporation, 15100 SW Koll Parkway, Beaverton, OR 97006; 800-274-5945. Suggested retail price for Super PC-KWIK: $79.95. Suggested retail price for Power Pak: $129.95

Norton Utilities. Symantec Corporation has incorporated disk caching in its Norton Utilities. Symantec Corporation, 10201 Torre Avenue, Cupertino, CA 95014; 800-441-7234. Suggested retail price: $179.

Windows. Microsoft Corporation has incorporated a disk caching program, SmartDrive, with its Windows Operating System. Microsoft Corporation, One Microsoft Way, Redmond, WA 98052; 800-426-9400. Suggested retail price: $149.95.

Solving System Compatibility Problems

Have you ever gotten the feeling that some of your programs don't like each other and maybe don't like your computer either? You try to run a program or use one of its advanced features, and nothing happens. Or you get some sort of error message. What you're experiencing is a compatibility problem.

One program won't work properly when another is running, usually because they're both trying to use the same part of your computer's system at the same time. It's not necessarily easy to solve this problem because you don't know which of these two programs are in conflict. It can take a lot of time-consuming detective work to first identify the other program, make the necessary changes, and then hope that you've not only solved this problem but that you haven't created another one as well.

To say the least, as PC programs have become more powerful, they've also become more sensitive about how they share the system's resources with the other programs or the computer itself. Whenever you add a new piece of software to your computer or install a piece of hardware, like a scanner, fax card, or CD-ROM, there's no guarantee that this new program or piece of hardware will get along with the other programs and hardware you already have on your system.

When this happens to me, I call customer support. The first thing they suggest is that we start the computer without loading any of my other programs except the newest one, the one that I'm having a problem with, to first determine if it's working properly or if it has a conflict with my computer.

To do this, it's necessary to edit my CONFIG.SYS and AUTOEXEC.BAT files, the two files that tell the computer what programs to load and in what order to load them, and temporarily suspend all the programs so that when I start the computer nothing is loaded. If the software works the way it's supposed to and the previous problem isn't reoccurring, then I know I've got a software conflict and not a hardware problem. Then they suggest that I reinstall each of my other programs, one at a time, to try and discover which one is causing the conflict.

So I must go back into my CONFIG.SYS and AUTOEXEC.BAT files, reactivate a program, restart my computer, and see what happens. I need to do this over and over until I'm able to pinpoint which two programs are in direct conflict.

As you can imagine, this process can be very time consuming and expensive, since I'm paying for the call to tech support and they're walking me through this process one step at a time. Then I read about a program called Bootcon.

Bootcon allows you to create and save many different configurations of your CONFIG.SYS and AUTOEXEC.BAT files and select whichever configuration you want when you start your computer.

When you need to take your computer's configuration apart to discover why something's not working, you just restart your computer, select a different system configuration, and start making your tests. When you eventually discover what needs to be changed, you make the permanent changes in the appropriate files, and you're done.

Bootcon also gives you more control over how your system uses its memory resources. Why load programs into memory if you're not going to use them? On my computer, I've got a flatbed scanner, a handheld scanner, and a CD-ROM. I found that I don't use these pieces of hardware at the same time, and may even go several days without using any of them. So I created separate configurations for each piece of hardware. When I want to use the scanner instead of the CD-ROM, I simply reboot my computer, select a new configuration, and I'm up and running in seconds.

Bootcon lets you create up to twenty-six different system configurations. Each configuration has a name and a description of up to 120 characters. When you start your computer, you can select a specific configuration from the Bootcon menu. If no selection is made, the default configuration is automatically loaded.

Bootcon. Modular Software Systems, 25826 104th Avenue SE, Kent, WA 98031; 800-438-3090. Suggested retail price: $79.

Improve Your Productivity by Upgrading Your Software

Every few years most software developers introduce an upgraded version of their products. Between upgrades, they listen to the comments, suggestions, and complaints of their customers and then try to give them what they want with their next product release. If you don't make it a point to upgrade your software, you're denying yourself the opportunity to take advantage of new features that not only can save you time but also can help you make more money.

As an example, WordPerfect Corporation (800-451-5151) recently introduced its latest version of WordPerfect, WordPerfect 6.0. In it they made more than six hundred changes or enhancements, improving what had been the computer world's best-selling word processor, WordPerfect 5.1. These changes were made because more than 30,000

WordPerfect users had requested them. The following is an extremely brief list of some of WordPerfect 6.0's enhancements:

- Color printing. WordPerfect now fully supports color printing on *all* color printers.
- Windowing. You can now open up to nine document screens at the same time, and move from one to another with the click of a mouse.
- Graphical interface. The graphics mode imitates a WYSIWYG (what you see is what you get) environment.
- Spreadsheet functions are built into tables. Many of the functions and cell formatting features that were formerly available only in spreadsheet programs can be accessed in WordPerfect 6.0.
- Fax. You can now send fax information directly from within WordPerfect.
- Envelopes with barcodes. The envelope feature creates an envelope using the mailing address in your current document. POSTNET barcodes can be automatically entered.

The list of enhancements can go on and on. Most important, if you don't take advantage of these improvements, you're going to find yourself working harder than you have to.

WordPerfect 6.0. WordPerfect Corporation, 1555 N. Technology Way, Orem, UT 84957; 800-451-5151. Suggested retail price: $495.

Get the Most Out of Technical Support in the Least Amount of Time

No matter how much you know about computers, you're always going to have to call technical support for the answer to a question. And when you call, you can expect to spend some time on hold, since most computer and software companies are understaffed. Here are some thoughts about how you can shorten both your hold time and the length of your call.

- Write down the technical support number in the front of the user's manual or highlight the number on the page where it's printed. Either bend a corner of the page or attach a Post-It note to it so you can find it quickly.
- Next to the number, you should also write down the serial number or user ID number of your product. When you're asked for this information, it'll be easily available.
- Every company has a computerized phone system that has many different choices. To save yourself time, write down the appropriate sequence of numbers to push, so your call can be quickly routed.
- The busiest times for technical support seem to be early in the morning, especially Monday morning, because everybody was trying to do something with their computer over the weekend and got into trouble. If you need to talk with technical support, try to do it first thing in the morning—not where you're located but where they're located—before everybody else tries to call. Use the different time zones to your best advantage.
- Don't call technical support during lunch hours, which is usually between eleven-thirty and one-thirty local time. During these hours, departments are generally understaffed, and you'll spend even more time waiting.
- If a company has recently started shipping a new product, you can expect the phone lines to technical support to be ringing off the hook because there will be thousands of users who have questions or problems. Call either very early in the morning or at the end of the day.
- As a rule, you should expect to wait for ten to fifteen minutes before you even talk to a technician, so make it a point to be doing something else while you're in line.

In addition to calling technical support when you've got a problem, it's often a good idea to call them to keep you from having a problem. If you're installing a new piece of software or doing something that's changing your system's configuration, first you should thoroughly read the installation manual. Then you should call technical support, tell them about your system, and ask them if there's anything else you should know or if there are some things you should—or shouldn't—be doing. Often they can give you some additional pieces of information that will help make the new program run better. I've found that thirty minutes on the phone has saved me what would have been many additional hours of headaches. Many times the technical support person will even walk you through the whole installation process.

And finally, don't make changes to your system at a time of day when you can't call technical support for help. It's a mistake to start taking your computer apart in the evenings or on the weekend, unless you're sure that you can put it back together again. You may find yourself upsetting your carefully designed system, and in a worst case scenario, you could find that because of a software conflict, your system's locked, you don't know how to get it started again, and technical support doesn't open until 8:00 A.M. on Monday, Pacific standard time.

Give Yourself a Guided Tour of Your Computer

If you've ever wanted to know how your computer works, or wanted additional information about certain devices or parts of a computer, then you'll love Computer Works. Computer Works is an interactive information system designed to let you explore the world of computers. Colorful animated graphics and comprehensive information highlight each component of the computer system, including the inner workings of computer monitors, disk drives, CD-ROM, mice, and other peripheral devices.

You can discover how your computer's central processing unit "thinks" and interacts with the main circuitry, explore the inside of the "motherboard"—the system unit's primary circuit board, and investigate the incredible storage capacity and advanced technology of the CD-ROM drive. Computer Works is available on disk and CD-ROM.

Computer Works. Software Marketing Corporation, 9830 South 51st Street Building A, Phoenix, AZ 85044; 800-545-6626. Suggested retail price: $79.95.

Part IV

WINNING THE FIGHT BETWEEN
YOU AND YOUR BODY

One of the side effects that people who work at a computer are experiencing are injuries to their hands, arms, back, and shoulders. Collectively, these injuries are called repetitive stress injuries, (RSI). These often result from a combination of things: The uninterrupted overuse of the hands and fingers through the repetitive motions of striking the computer keyboard and the position of the body in relationship to the keyboard.

You may not be experiencing any pain or discomfort of any kind at this moment, but I feel it's important for you to become aware of the possibility that you, too, could suffer an injury that could easily be avoided. What begins as a sore arm, with a dull aching sensation, could develop into a more serious injury if your working environment or work habits remain unchanged—or if the injury is left untreated.

What Are We Doing to Our Hands?

With today's powerful computers and ever-expanding list of productivity-improving software, we're spending more time at the keyboard and aren't giving our hands the opportunity to take a break. In the past, we used to perform many different activities in the office, but with the increased use of the computer all that has changed. The modern office has left many of us with little variation in our daily tasks. There is no paper to put into the printer, no ribbons to change, no corrections to make with Wite-Out.

If we need to check the spelling of a word, we don't pull out a dictionary, we run the spell checker. When we need a copy of a letter, we don't get up from our chair, go to the file cabinet, search for the file folder, pull out the piece of paper, and then walk down the hall to the office copier. We search through our computer directories, find the file, bring it onto the screen, and push the PRINT button. We never leave our seat.

When you send a memo, you no longer write it on a carbonized three-part form. You either type it in your word processor and print three copies—or you send the memo electronically over your E-mail network. Because of all this new technology, your hands and fingers, back, neck, and shoulders never get a rest. Even when you pick up the phone to make a call, you use the same finger and hand motion to push down the telephone's keys that you use when you're typing at the keyboard.

You may not think your hands are doing *that* much work, but they *really* are getting an extensive workout from the keyboard. For example, if a person spends five hours a day typing at the rate of sixty words (360 keystrokes) per minute, that's 100,000 keystrokes a day, 500,000 keystrokes a week, and 25,000,000 keystrokes a year. Cut it down to forty words per minute for only three hours a day, and you've still got more than 43,000 keystrokes a day, and 215,000 keystrokes a week. In addition, your body isn't moving, because you're sitting in the same chair for hours at a time.

To compound the problem, much of this work is done by the little fingers. They are used to pressing and holding the SHIFT, CONTROL, ALT, RETURN, BACK SPACE, and TAB keys, in addition to the letters that are assigned to them. For many people the motion used to press these keys is unnatural because the wrist is bending left and right at the same time that the fingers are reaching for these keys. When done for hours at a time, day after day, the muscles and tendons in the fingers, hands, and arms become susceptible to injury.

How Your Hands Work

The muscles in the forearm, through long thin fibers called tendons, control the movement of the fingers. The tendons, along with blood vessels and nerves, run through the small carpal bones of the wrist. This narrow wrist channel is called the carpal tunnel. With normal finger and hand motions, the tendons easily slide past each other as they pass through the carpal tunnel. However, should the fingers or hands do too much repetitive work, especially if the wrist is cocked, the tendons will begin to rub against one another.

Once this happens, the tendons become inflamed and begin to swell. This swelling often takes place inside the carpal tunnel because that's where the tendons are most likely to rub against one another. If the swelling continues, the tendons will begin to press against the median nerve.

The median nerve controls the movement and feelings of the first three fingers and the thumb. If the median nerve becomes irritated, it too will begin to swell. The compression of the nerve causes it to misfire, which is usually felt as a tingling sensation in the hands and fingers. This is one of the early signs of what is commonly called carpal tunnel syndrome. Without proper medical attention this condition can create a feeling of numbness in the hands and a loss of fine motor control in the fingers.

Symptoms of Repetitive Stress Injuries

A repetitive stress injury is a term generally used to describe an injury that occurs as a result of repetitive motions. Carpal tunnel syndrome is a repetitive stress injury. A person who is suffering from a repetitive stress injury may feel pain in the hands and forearms. This could be felt as a throbbing, tingling, or burning sensation. Many people have found their symptoms are often worse at night and in the early morning than during the workday. In severe cases a person may have difficulty holding and grasping objects and be unable to make a fist.

If the work environment that contributed to this injury remains unchanged and the injury itself is not treated, the physical problems can spread from the hands and wrist to the shoulders, neck, and back. It can eventually become a crippling injury. What I have just described is a worst case scenario. This outcome can easily be avoided simply by making some minor changes in your work environment.

Creating a Healthy Work Environment

We all come in different shapes and sizes—some of us are tall, others are short, one person may have large hands, another person's hands may be small and petite. Because of this, you need to be able to adjust your work area to fit your own physical needs. To create a working environment that is right for you, there are a number of different factors that must be taken into consideration: the height of your desk, chair, and keyboard; the position of the monitor; and the intensity of the interior lighting under which you're working. If your office equipment is forcing you to sit in an unnatural position—especially if your wrists are cocked—the risk of injury is greatly increased.

Up until now, you've probably never given any thought as to how you should position yourself at the keyboard. Most people position the height of their chair so their feet rest comfortably on the floor without any regard to the position of their hands in relation to the keyboard. A better way is to make sure your hands are properly positioned at the keyboard—then make any other necessary adjustments.

Position Your Hands Properly on the Keyboard

When sitting at the keyboard, you want to type with a flat wrist, positioned at or just below elbow level, so that your forearms are at a 90-degree angle to your upper arms. Your arms should rest comfortably at your sides; your wrists should be relaxed; and your fingers

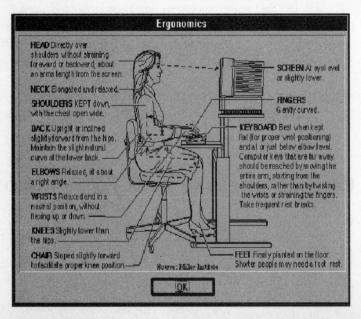

should be gently curved. Typing with a cocked wrist, either upward or downward, places extra stress on the tendons and nerves as they pass through the wrist. This wrist position is often the result of a person sitting in a chair that is either too high or too low in relation to the keyboard.

If the height of the keyboard is adjustable, it's easy to achieve this 90-degree position. If the keyboard is sitting on a desk or table whose height cannot be changed, you can compensate for this by raising your chair to the proper height and using a footrest to support your feet.

If the keyboard is too large for your hands or fingers, try to reach the outlying keys by lifting your hand and arm, from the shoulder, rather than twisting your wrists or straining to reach those keys with your fingers.

When typing, avoid resting your wrists on the edge of the work surface. Doing so can put additional pressure on those same tendons and nerves that you're trying to treat so gingerly. To reduce the strain on your wrists, muscles, and tendons, consider using a padded wrist or palm rest that you can place in front of the keyboard. A wrist rest can be especially helpful during brief typing breaks. And when typing, keep your hands relaxed, type gently, and don't pound the keys.

Position Your Monitor So You Don't Have to Lean Forward

Once you've discovered the proper position for your body in relation to the keyboard, you need to address the position of your monitor. The top of the monitor should be positioned so that it's even with or slightly below your forehead. Now you can look straight at the screen without being forced to tilt your head forward and downward.

Books or a monitor support arm can be used to raise your monitor to the desired height. These arms allow the monitor to "float" above the desktop and offer tremendous flexibility because you can position them at any height and distance from your eyes that you want.

You also want to position your monitor in such a way as to minimize on-screen glare. If it's impossible to find such a position, place an antiglare screen on the monitor or attach a visorlike hood over the top.

To make the task of typing easier and, at the same time, reduce the strain on your neck, attach a copy holder to the side of your monitor. The copy holder holds the papers right next to the screen, minimizing eye and neck movement. This allows you to look at your text and then the screen by slightly turning your head left or right—instead of having to lean forward while raising your head up and down.

A Footrest Improves the Circulation of Blood Throughout Your Body

A footrest is an important—and often overlooked—piece of office furniture. It can reduce the pressure on the back of your thighs, minimize lower back strain, and by raising your feet, improve the circulation of blood throughout your body. Most important, it compensates for the lack of flexibility between your chair and your desk. By supporting your legs and feet, it allows you to sit higher than would normally be comfortable.

Office Equipment That Reduces Stress on the Body

Sit in a Chair That Fits Your Body

A well-designed chair is one that adjusts to the shape of your body and allows you to find comfortable positions while you're working. Once it is properly adjusted, it not only supports your back but also reduces the strain on your shoulders, neck, arms, and hands. These are some of the features you should look for in a chair:

- The seat height should be easily adjustable upward and downward. When sitting at your desk, your elbows should be at the same height as the keyboard. If the keyboard is sitting on the desktop, your seat will probably need to be raised higher than you're normally accustomed to. As a result, your feet will no longer be resting comfortably on the floor. To compensate for this, you'll need a footrest to support your feet. If the keyboard height is adjustable, then you can lower the height of your seat so your feet will comfortably reach the floor.

- The backrest should be adjustable up and down and fit the curve of your lower back. You want your back to be fully supported so you can sit up straight, with your head positioned directly over your shoulders. Your arms should be resting comfortably at your sides. If you need additional back support, use cushions or foam padding.

- The seat cushion should have a slight forward slope and shouldn't dig into the back of your legs. This takes the pressure off the spine and transfers it to the thighs and feet.

- The arms should be adjustable so you can change the height and angle of each arm, allowing the chair to conform to the shape of your body.

- The chair should swivel left and right, tilt forward and backward, and roll on casters. These features give you more mobility and ease of motion, making that task of trying to reach something much easier.

The Most Comfortable Office Chair I Have Ever Used

It took me several weeks of research to determine what features a person should look for when purchasing an office chair. And then I got a Criterion chair from Steelcase. I kid you not, every feature that I have just described has been incorporated into the Criterion chair. It is by far the most comfortable office chair I have ever used.

Fitting the chair to both the job and to the body of the person who is using it can be quite a challenge. And Steelcase has not only included every possible adjustment in its Criterion chair, it has also made the adjustments very easy to use. The chair goes up and down, swivels left and right, and is supported on five casters. The height of the back support is adjustable so you can fit the back support to the small of your back. The back support tilts backward, or with a flick of the toggle switch it can be locked in place. For the person who likes to lean forward when working, there is an adjustment that allows the seat pan to tilt forward.

The features that I like the most are the individually adjustable armrests, which are designed to support the hands and forearms. When you're typing, your hands aren't resting on the keyboard. Instead they're floating over the keyboard. To change the height of the armrest, which is adjustable over a four-inch range, you squeeze and hold a narrow bar located at the front of the armrest, reposition it to the desired height, and release the bar. There is another adjustment that allows you to move each armrest closer to your body so your arms can be comfortably supported while typing.

When I had positioned the chair so that my arms were at a 90-degree angle to the keyboard I found that I had to make some other adjustments. I needed a footrest to support my feet, and I needed to raise the height of the monitor a good six inches because I found that the top of the monitor was now at chin level instead of being at the level of my eyebrows.

I can honestly say that my Criterion chair has gotten a lot of use. To complete this book I found myself sitting at the computer for ten, twelve or more hours a day, seven days a week, for almost two months. I would set my alarm for 5:00 A.M. every morning so I could work for a few hours before breakfast, and I would often continue working after dinner. Yes, I did get an occasional stiff neck, but I can assure you it would have been impossible for me to spend so many hours at the computer in a chair that wasn't as well designed as the Criterion.

Criterion Chairs. Steelcase Inc., Grand Rapids, MI 49501. Criterion chairs come with either a high back or a midback. The armrests are optional. For a catalog and a current price list call 800-333-9939.

Improve Your Vision with a New Monitor

The size and resolution of your monitor will also make a difference to your eyes, neck, and back. If you have to overconcentrate to read your monitor, because of either low resolution or small screen size, the muscles in your neck and shoulders become tense—and you'll become fatigued quite quickly.

If you're using an older monitor, one with a fourteen-inch screen and a resolution of 640 × 480, your eyes may be working harder than they should. The screen's probably too small for your needs. With the lower resolution, the characters aren't clear, especially if you're using Windows. You should give a lot of thought to upgrading to a fifteen- or seventeen-inch monitor with a resolution of at least 1024 × 768.

When I upgraded my computer I replaced my old monitor with a Nanao fifteen-inch color monitor. I didn't know what I had been missing until I plugged it into my computer and turned it on. The first things I noticed were the increase in size, clarity, and brightness. My old fourteen-inch monitor had a viewing area of about sixty-three square inches (seven by nine) with a resolution of 640 × 480 (4,900 pixels per square inch). (The number of picture elements, pixels, per square inch defines the degree of detail in an image.)

The Nanao's viewing area is 88 square inches (eleven by eight), an increase of almost 40 percent, and the resolution is 1024 × 768 (almost 9,000 pixels per square inch), which translates into much greater screen clarity. The flat screen has a nonglare, antireflective coating, so I no longer need a "visor" to keep glare off my screen. Furthermore, the WideView screen provides an edge-to-edge viewing area.

I didn't realize until after I changed monitors how much I was straining to read my screen because of the small size of the screen itself and the lower resolution. Now I know how a person feels when they come back from the eye doctor with a new prescription for eyeglasses. I can see clearly again. In fact I no longer need to have the monitor so close to me.

There are some other features I would like to mention. The picture and color controls are located at the front of the screen, making adjustments easy, and I liked being able to adjust the size, position, and centering of the display area. There is also an energy-saving feature. Whenever the computer isn't in use, screen saver becomes active, reducing the monitor's power consumption to about 7 percent of normal.

Nanao USA Corporation. 23535 Telo Avenue, Torrance, CA 90505. Nanao makes a complete line of high- and ultrahigh-resolution color monitors from fifteen inches to twenty-one inches in size. For a catalog and a current price list call 800-800-5202.

If You've Been Experiencing Discomfort, Try a Different Type of Keyboard

If you've been experiencing discomfort in your fingers, hands, or arms, in addition to getting a new chair or monitor, you may want to try changing the keyboard itself. The layout of the standard QWER-TY keyboard doesn't really take the human body into consideration. Everything is laid out straight and flat, and, depending upon how you sit at the keyboard, your fingers may be forced to stretch to reach specific keys while the wrist is bent at an unnatural angle.

As noted, the fifth finger comes under the most strain because of the longer stretches needed to reach many of its keys. In addition, the CRTL, ALT, and SHIFT keys need to be held down while other keys are being pressed, and the act of holding down a key can cause additional stress on your fingers.

With these keyboard limitations in mind, several companies are now designing new keyboards that take into consideration the construction of the human body. As a result, they are making typing much easier on the hands, wrists, and arms.

Because I spend so much time at the keyboard, I've been experiencing pain and discomfort in my left arm for many months. I can attest that my discomfort has greatly subsided since I started using both of the following keyboards. If you're experiencing any type of pain or discomfort in your hands, wrists, or arms, these are both good keyboards for you to try.

Marquardt-Miniergo Keyboard

The Marquardt-MiniErgo keyboard took just a few hours of use before I adjusted to it. Within a few days, I felt very comfortable using it. The keys have been divided into two angled, V-shaped sections that are placed three inches apart. The keyboard gently slopes to the sides and front to help align the hands and wrists with the arms, thus reducing strain. This enables typing with a natural posture of the hands and therefore reduces stress factors for muscles and joints. There is a generous three-inch-wide resting area, just below the keys, where the palms of your hands can rest when you want to take a quick break.

Several keys have been placed in between the two V-sections for use by the index finger or thumb. These keys are the INSERT, DELETE, and the four ARROW KEYS. The PAGE UP, PAGE DOWN, HOME, and END keys share the arrow keys and become active when an additional function key is held down. Each keyboard section has its own space bar.

Marquardt-Miniergo Keyboard. Marquardt Switches, 2711 Route 20 East, Cazenovia, NY 13035; 315-655-8050. Suggested retail price: $179.

The Kinesis Ergonomic Keyboard

The Kinesis Ergonomic Keyboard is a fantastic keyboard! I have really enjoyed using it. The keyboard has been completely redesigned with the human body and hands in mind. The designers have given a lot of thought and consideration as to how the human hand and body relate to the keyboard. They repositioned the keys that were formally pressed with the little finger—the BACK SPACE, DELETE, CTRL, ALT, HOME, END, PAGE UP, PAGE DOWN, ENTER, and SPACE keys—and created two sets of thumb pads. Now the thumb, which is much stronger and durable, can do the work that had previously been assigned to the little fingers. Then they added a foot pedal that can be used in place of the SHIFT key, which takes further strain off your little finger. (A second, programmable foot pedal is also available.)

The Kinesis Ergonomic Keyboard looks more like the control panel of a spaceship than a computer keyboard. The keyboard is divided into two concave wells that are placed six inches apart. This separates the hands, allowing the elbows and arms to rest at shoulder width. Because the hands are separated, there is less twisting of the wrist when typing.

Because your fingers are different lengths the designers then positioned the keys in a slight arc, instead of in a straight line—thus conforming the keyboard to the shape of the hand. This configuration allows you to type with a flat wrist and slightly curved fingers and eliminates excessive reaching by the little fingers. Because the keys are laid out vertically rather than horizontally, you are able to curl or extend your fingers to reach a specific key instead of being required to turn your wrists horizontally or diagonally. With the placement of the keys inside the curve of the wells, the keys are closer to your fingers than they would be on a flat keyboard.

There is also a keyboard remapping feature. This feature allows you to customize the keyboard to fit your specific needs by giving you the ability to change the position of specific keys on the keyboard. If, for instance, you don't want to press the TAB key with your fifth finger, you can remap the keys so the CTRL + T key has the same function as the TAB key. Now you can use your index fingers to move the cursor to the next tab position, instead of striking the TAB key with your fifth finger.

Macros can also be programmed into the keyboard. The Kinesis keyboard stores approximately 2KB of information in onboard memory. If you frequently repeat a series of keystrokes, you can record them into a macro and save yourself the time and effort of retyping the same characters over and over.

If you've been experiencing discomfort, the Kinesis Ergonomic Keyboard is certainly worth trying.

Kinesis Ergonomic Keyboard. Kinesis Corporation, 915 118th Avenue Southeast, Bellevue, WA 98005; 800-454-6374. Suggested retail price $390.

With a Trackball You Can Operate Your Computer with Your Fingertips

If you would like an alternative to using a mouse, you should try Kensington's Expert Mouse Trackball. Its ergonomic design offers you maximum keyboard comfort while it gives you precision control over your cursor's movement. And because a trackball remains stationary—you only move the ball, not the entire device—it doesn't take up much desktop space.

The Expert Mouse's large trackball, which is almost the size of a billiard ball, is easily controlled by your fingertips and offers very smooth cursor movement. The buttons, which are placed symmetrically on each side of the ball, have a light easy-to-press feel and accommodate both left-and right-handed users. The real beauty of the Expert Mouse is in the software. It has several user-programmable functions that give you the ability to adjust and modify how the cursor responds to the movement of the trackball.

Custom Acceleration

The Custom Acceleration feature allows you to adjust the cursor acceleration, the speed that your cursor moves in relation to how far and how quickly you move the trackball. With a single setting you can have both a slow and a fast cursor movement. Move the ball slowly and there is very little acceleration. This gives you precise control and is especially helpful when you're doing detailed work. Move the ball quickly and the cursor will zip from one area of the screen to the other.

Brilliant Cursor

Kensington's Brilliant Cursor technology is the latest in advanced cursor control. With the single click of a trackball button you can have your cursor jump to different predefined points, HotSpots, on your screen. The Brilliant Cursor is very useful because it can get you to frequently used on-screen areas, such as file and edit menus, or color palettes very quickly.

Slow Cursor

The Slow Cursor technology allows you to move your cursor very slowly and precisely. It offers ultraprecision control so you can have pixel-by-pixel cursor movement, and when you need very accurate pointing, the cursor movement can be locked in either an x-(horizontal) or y- (vertical) axis. This is especially useful for placing graphics, drawings, or page layouts in exact locations on screen.

Enhanced Programmable Mouse Buttons

The Programmable Mouse button commands allow you to customize and automate the Windows functions you use most often. They enable you to program and execute different keyboard commands or send a group of keystrokes to the computer. They can even be used to launch macros.

I've been using an Expert Mouse trackball for several years and have found it easy to use. With Kensington's programmable cursor software, I've been able to customize my mouse to fit my style of work.

Expert Mouse. Kensington Microware Limited, 2855 Campus Drive, San Mateo, CA 94403; 800-535-4242. Suggested retail price: $149.95.

TrakMate: The Wristpad with the Trackball

Many people find it desirable to have a wristpad to support their hands when they want to take a quick break from typing. Key Tronic has taken the idea one step further. Their TrakMate is a free-standing, adjustable wristpad with an integrated trackball that is conveniently centered in front of the space bar. You use your thumb and finger to move the cursor without ever taking your hands away from the keyboard. On either side of the trackball are two large buttons that function as the left and right buttons on a two-button mouse. Additional buttons provide drag lock and speed control.

If you're someone who feels that it's a lot of wasted motion to take your hands away from the keyboard whenever you need to use your mouse, you'll find the TrakMate to be a great productivity-improvement tool.

TrakMate: The Wristpad with the Trackball. Key Tronic, P.O. Box 14687, Spokane, WA 99214, 800-262-6006. Suggested retail price: $149.

If You Can't Type, Let Your Computer Take Dictation

If you do have a serious repetitive stress injury, you may be interested in a software product that converts speech to editable computer text. DragonDictate's speech recognition software makes it possible for people to talk to their computers—dictating text and data—instead of typing. Basically, the user dictates into a headset, handheld, or wireless microphone, and the words appear on the screen as they are spoken.

DragonDictate has the ability to control the MS-DOS operating system, the Windows graphical interface, and the most popular word processing, spreadsheet, and database programs, including Microsoft Word, WordPerfect, Lotus 1-2-3, Quicken, and dBase. For example, in WordPerfect the command to save a file is the F7 key. When a user says the command phrase "save file," WordPerfect thinks the F7 key was pressed. DragonDictate can also be used with your LAN, E-mail, and faxing software.

The program normally produces text at the rate of about 35 words a minute, but with voice macros that automate the insertion of familiar words, phrases, and titles, it's possible to increase the effective rate to 100 words per minute. The program comes with a large 30,000-word active vocabulary and a 120,000-word backup dictionary to access job-related words. You can also add to the program proper names, jargon, or any words or phrases suited to your specific needs. DragonDictate's patented speaker-adaptation features allow the program to learn your voice, and with increased usage it becomes accustomed to your vocabulary and speaking style.

DragonDictate. Dragon Systems, Inc., 320 Nevada Street, Newton, MA 02160; 800-825-5897. Suggested retail price: $4,995.

Improve Your Productivity by Using a Telephone Headset

One productivity-improving product that I think everybody should have is a telephone headset. I've been using one for years and have found that it's greatly improved my productivity. Originally I purchased a headset because my neck was getting sore from cradling the handset between my ear, chin, and shoulder. I also found it very difficult to take notes while I was on the phone. I just couldn't find an easy way to hold the phone to my left ear, use my left elbow to hold the pad of paper still, try to write with my right hand, and remain comfortable—all at the same time.

Once I started using the headset, I was not only comfortable, but I also discovered that my efficiency with the phone increased. I was able to dial more calls during the day and could answer the phone in a fewer number of rings. Best of all, the party at the other end of the line never knew I wasn't using a traditional handset, nor did I have to resort to using the speaker phone, which many people find annoying.

If you spend much time on the phone, a headset is a great way to improve your productivity. You can use both hands to take written notes of your conversation or type information from the keyboard. You can also answer a call more quickly because you only have to pick up the receiver. You don't have to bring it to your ear.

Best of all, you no longer have to hold your neck and head in an awkward position as you try to cradle the receiver between your ear, shoulder, and chin in order to free your hands. Headsets have padded ear pieces, so you'll never again experience the discomfort of the handset's ear piece as it presses against your ear during a long telephone conversation. Now you can concentrate on the conversation instead of on the pain in your neck or the tenderness in your ear. That alone can save you a great deal of discomfort and perhaps a trip to the chiropractor.

Today's headsets are light and comfortable. Once you put one on, you'll quickly forget that you're even wearing it. There are a number of different choices in headsets. There are ultralight behind-the-ear headsets that weigh just half an ounce, as well as headsets with adjustable headbands that fit over the top of your head. You can select a headset that provides sound in either one ear or both ears.

Plantronics makes a full line of headsets for both the corporate user and the person who runs a business out of their home.

Plantronics. 345 Encinal Street, Santa Cruz, CA 95060. For a catalog and a current price list call 800-426-5858.

Footrests, Wristrests, Back Cushions, and More

There are a number of companies that carry a complete line of products designed to improve your productivity and make your workspace more comfortable. These would include footrests, wristrests, back cushions, and copy holders that attach to the side of your monitor.

BackCare Corporation of Chicago, IL (312-258-0888); Chase Ergonomics of Albuquerque, NM (800-621-5436); Curtis Manufacturing, Inc., of Jaffrey, NH (800-955-5544); Details, of New York City (212-334-9100); and Ergodyne of Saint Paul, MN (800-225-8238). These all offer a full line of computer and office accessories, including footrests, wristrests, back cushions, VDT support arms, and articulating keyboard trays. BackCare Corporation also carries a full line of ergonomically designed chairs.

If you're looking for office furniture, Steelcase of Grand Rapids, MI (800-333-9939), carries a complete line of furniture, including desks, chairs, and filing cabinets.

Take Care of Your Hands and Your Body

We all spend too much time sitting at the keyboard and not enough time moving around or stretching. Before you start typing, and throughout the day, it's a good idea to do a few exercises that will warm up, relax, and stretch the muscles in your hands and fingers. Here are some stretching exercises that will help you get through the day.

- Hand massage. Gently massage the palms of your hands and fingers for thirty to sixty seconds each.

- Lower forearm stretch. To stretch the underside of your forearm, turn your palm facing up and, with your other hand, gently press your fingers away from your body until you feel your muscles begin to stretch. Hold for five seconds, then relax. Repeat three to five times.
- Upper forearm stretch. To stretch the topside of your forearm, make a fist, and with your other hand, press it toward your body until you feel your muscles begin to stretch. Hold for five seconds, then relax. Repeat three to five times.
- Wrist circles. Hold your arms away from your sides and slowly rotate both wrists ten times in each direction, as if you were drawing circles with your fingertips.
- Five finger stretch and fist squeezes. Spread the fingers of both hands far apart and hold for two seconds, then make your hands into a fist and hold the fist for two seconds. Repeat three to five times.

Don't Sit Still, Energize Your Body

The human body was designed to move, and you shouldn't stay seated in the same position at the keyboard for hours on end. If you stay seated for too long, your muscles get stiff, you become fatigued, and your productivity begins to decline.

At a minimum, make it a point every ten to fifteen minutes to shift your weight from one side to the other and reposition your body on your chair. This will help you combat fatigue and improve the circulation of your blood.

The following are a few exercise that will stretch your tired muscles and get your blood flowing again. Within a few minutes you'll feel refreshed and invigorated. These should be done at least once in the morning and again in the afternoon.

- The whole body stretch. Stand up, raise your hands above your head, and try to touch the ceiling. For variation, try to touch the ceiling with one hand at a time. Hold the stretch for five to ten seconds. Repeat several times.

- Back stretch. Hold your arms straight out from your sides, and with your palms forward, take a deep breath and push your hands gently backward. Hold the stretch three to five seconds and exhale. Repeat the stretch three to five times. This exercise will help you to stand up straight and get rid of your rounded shoulders.
- Shoulder roll. To loosen up your shoulders, stand up and pretend you're swimming the backstroke. First bring one arm backward, and then the other. Repeat three to five times.
- Shoulder shrug. Slowly lift your shoulders toward your ears, then roll them backward and down again, making a complete circle. Repeat three to five times.
- Shoulder blade squeeze. Stand up straight, clasp your hands behind your head, and squeeze your shoulder blades together. Take a deep breath and as you exhale, allow your muscles to relax.
- Neck stretches. Straighten and arch your back, sit up straight, and hold your head high. Relax your neck by lifting your head and gently try to touch your right ear to your right shoulder, stretching the muscles on the left side of your neck. Let your head roll down to the center, rest a moment, and pick up your head again. Now try to touch your left ear to your left shoulder and let your head roll down to the center, then pick it up. Repeat this two or three times.

Keep Yourself Healthy

Take at least one fifteen-minute break every two hours and try not to type continuously for more than thirty minutes at a time without taking at least a few moments to do something else. Switch to another activity that uses the hands differently. Remember, the hands' natural position is with the thumb turned upward, the gesture you use when you reach out to shake someone's hand. So make it a point to take your hands off the keyboard every fifteen or twenty minutes and shake them for a few moments. And finally, since there are many things we do at the keyboard that are repetitive, we should use the computer to automate those keystrokes with a macro. Keyboard macros will not only reduce the wear and tear on your hands and fingers, but they will also make you much more productive because the computer can play back a series of recorded keystrokes much faster than you can type them. For more information on macros see a complete explanation on page 167.

Software to Keep You Healthy

Because of increasing awareness of proper health and physical fitness several software companies have now come out with products that will remind you to take a break from your keyboard, provide you with detailed medical information, help you to analyze your medical insurance coverages, prepare the claim forms for submission to your insurance company, and keep track of your calories if you're trying to lose weight.

Take an Exercise Break

Exercise Break is a program designed to remind you to take a break from your keyboard work. It was created by a team of healthcare professionals to help you reduce the muscle tension caused by spending too many hours at the PC.

The program loads automatically when you turn on your computer and then pops up at regular intervals to remind you that it's time to take a break. When the program pops up, you are walked through a series of stretching exercises. The beautifully illustrated animated graphics, with on-screen instructions, act like an aerobics instructor as they show you how to do each set of exercises one at a time. A timer shows you how long a stretch should be held, and the program "beeps" when it's time to do the next stretch.

You can select from a list of different stretches. There are a series of exercises for the hands, wrist, face, neck, shoulders, back, and legs. The program is very flexible. You select which exercises you want to

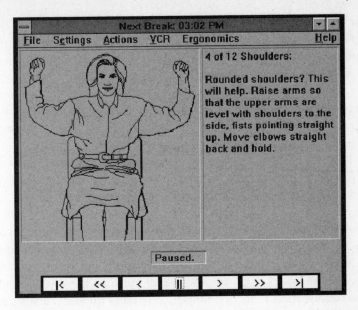

do, the sequence you want to do them in, and the length of time for each stretch. If you're too engrossed in your present work and are not ready to take a break when the program pops up, you can cancel the current session or postpone it for a few minutes.

The program includes an ergonomic posture chart and separate checklists for your work environment, your work area, monitor, keyboard, chair, and posture. I set the program to remind me to stretch every hour, which I like very much. I need to be reminded regularly that it's time to take a break, get away from the keyboard, and stretch my tired body. After just a few minutes of stretching, I feel invigorated and ready to go back to work.

Exercise Break. Hopkins Technology, 421 Hazel Lane, Hopkins, MN 55343; 800-397-9211. Suggested retail price $29.95.

Use Your Computer to Take a More Active Role in Managing Your Health

HealthDesk is an information management and health education program designed to help you take a more active role in managing your health. HealthDesk helps you track information about your personal medical history and health activities and provides general information about how the human body works.

With HealthDesk's medical records–keeping facilities, you can keep detailed records of yourself and each member of your family. These can include dates of doctor visits, a list of your vaccinations, a log of any medication you may be taking, and a complete listing of medical expenses that you have incurred.

HealthDesk's Health Managers act as electronic notebooks that let you log and keep track of your progress for such activities as your daily exercise, reducing your cholesterol levels, or trying to lose weight.

As you manage your personal data in HealthDesk, you can also take advantage of its extensive links to a wide range of health education topics, then use the Resource Guide to obtain the names, numbers, and addresses of organizations that can provide you with additional information about any subject you find of interest. HealthDesk's colorful information-packed graphics and lively animations make health management fun for everybody.

HealthDesk. HealthDesk Corporation, 1801 Fifth Street, Berkeley, CA 94701; 800-578-5767. Suggested retail price $99.95.

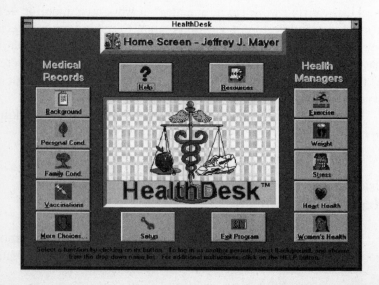

Use Your Computer to Manage Your Health Insurance

One thing that everybody hates to do is to fill out and submit medical bills to their insurance company. It's a tedious and time-consuming process. Once the bills are filed, it takes a lot of time and effort to try to keep track of the status of the claim as it progresses. Now there's a computer program, Med$ure, that will do it for you.

Med$ure will help you keep track of your medical bills and the status of all your claims, record benefits you receive from your insurance company, and itemize the expenses that you must pay yourself. The program makes it easy for you to keep all the medical information about yourself and your family as well as the basic information about all your health care providers. As medical expenses are incurred, the bills are entered into Med$ure along with a complete explanation of what happened, what was done by the doctor, and why. When the time comes to submit a claim, this information can be printed out on a standard, universally accepted medical claim form. You can also maintain a personal health history for each member of your family, including such things as accidents, injuries, hospitalizations, and allergies; a record of all your immunizations; height and weight graphs; and a family medical tree.

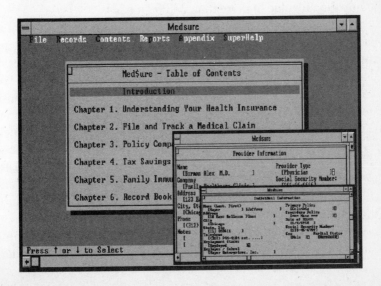

Med$ure takes the mystery out of health insurance. The program reads like a book, with chapters and subchapters that give a complete and thorough explanation of every provision in a medical insurance policy. And if you're thinking of replacing your existing coverages, Med$ure can help you compare the different policies so you can select the one that is best for you.

Med$ure. Time Solutions, 45 Kellers Farm Road, Easton, CT 06612; 800-552-3302. Suggested retail price $69.95.

Use Your Computer to Control Your Weight

Have you ever tried to lose weight, keep track of your diet, or analyze the nutritional content of the foods you eat? Santé is an all-in-one weight control, diet planning, exercise, and recipe program. This computer program makes it easy for you to stay healthy, fit, control your weight, and still get the vitamins, minerals, and nutrients you need from any food available in your grocery store, restaurant, or garden. The program has nutritional information on over 2,300 foods, 500 brand name foods, and the individual menu items offered at several major restaurant chains, including McDonald's, Burger King, Burger Chef, and Domino's Pizza. (The CD-ROM version analyzes the nutritional value of more than 23,000 foods.)

When you want to lose weight, you must burn up more calories than you consume, and Santé gives you the ability to use your computer to keep track of both the calories you eat and the number of calories you burn up every day. To keep track of your calories, you record everything you ate during the day. Once this information is entered into the computer, you can view, or print, a report that shows the calories, vitamins, and minerals provided by a single food, a single meal, or everything you ate. Santé can also give you a report that analyzes the caloric and nutritional breakdown of any food in the database. Then you enter all the activities you did during the day, and Santé calculates the number of calories you burned, using a caloric consumption list of more than two hundred exercises and activities.

And finally, have you ever wanted to get all of your recipes into your computer? Santé has an extensive list of recipes, and by adding your own, you can turn your computer into a cookbook. Print a hard copy of your favorite recipe and you can begin cooking a delicious meal in minutes. With Santé, it's like having a dietitian and weight control counselor in your computer.

Santé. Hopkins Technology, 421 Hazel Lane, Hopkins, MN 55343; 800-397-9211. Suggested retail price $59.95.

A Few Final Thoughts

To say the least, I've had a lot of fun writing this book. I had no idea that there were so many timesaving, productivity-improving software programs available, and I had a wonderful time testing all of them. When I first started thinking about writing a book on productivity improvement, the computer was to be a part of the book, but not the entire book. But once I began doing my research, the complete focus changed. Everywhere I looked I found another piece of software that would help a person do a task quicker, faster, and better. Before I knew it I was writing a book on computer software, and the length of the book kept growing and growing.

The glue that holds everything together is Microsoft's Windows. Windows has created an environment where you can use your computer to do your work, not just the individual programs that are running on your computer. With multitasking you can have several programs running at once; the Windows Clipboard makes it easy to move information from one program to another; and since all of the programs use the same basic structure, once you've learned how to use one program, it's easy to learn how to use a second one.

In today's highly competitive business world, you need every productivity-improving, cost-reducing tool that is available, and with the new Windows software, it's easy to stay one step ahead of the competition, get more work done in less time and with less effort, improve the quality of the work you do, and make more money. Now you're being efficient, effective, and productive.

APPENDIX

Appendix

Read a Computer Magazine to Learn About the Newest Productivity-Improving Software

I learned about many of the software products that were discussed in this book by reading computer magazines. I've found that thumbing through a stack of computer magazines is a great way to pass the time during a long flight or during a layover. On your next business trip, pick up a magazine and look through it. You'll be amazed at the number of new hardware and software products that are available. The following is a list of the major PC magazines:

Byte
McGraw-Hill, Inc.
One Phoenix Mill Lane
Peterborough, NH 03458
Editorial: 603-924-9281
Subscriptions: 800-257-9402

CD-ROM World
Meckler Corporation
11 Ferry Lane West
Westport, CT 06880
Editorial and subscriptions:
203-226-6967

Computer Buyer's Guide and Handbook
Bedford Communications, Inc.
150 Fifth Avenue
New York, NY 10011
Editorial: 212-807-8220
Subscriptions: 800-877-5487

Home Office Computing
Scholastic, Inc.
730 Broadway
New York, NY 10003
Editorial: 212-505-3580
Subscriptions: 800-288-7812

Info World
Info World Publishing Company
155 Bovet Road
San Mateo, CA 94402
Editorial and subscriptions:
415-572-7341.

Laptop Buyer's Guide and Handbook
Bedford Communications, Inc.
150 Fifth Avenue
New York, NY 10011
Editorial: 212-807-8220
Subscriptions: 800-877-5487

Mobile Office
CurtCo Publishing
Warner Plaza V
21800 Oxnard Street
Suite 250
Woodland Hills, CA 91367
Editorial and subscriptions: 818-
593-6100.

Online Access
Chicago Fine Print, Inc.
920 North Franklin
Chicago, IL 60610
Editorial and subscriptions: 312-
573-1700.

PC Computing
Ziff Communications Company
950 Tower Lane
20th Floor
Roster City, CA 94404
Editorial: 415-578-7000
Subscriptions: 800-322-8229

PC Magazine
Ziff-Davis Publishing Company
One Park Avenue
New York, NY 10016
Editorial: 212-503-5255
Subscriptions: 800-289-0429

PC World
501 Second Street
Suite 600
San Francisco, CA 94107
Editorial: 415-243-0500
Subscriptions: 800-234-3498

PC Laptop Computers
9171 Wilshire Boulevard
Suite 300
Los Angeles, CA 90210
Editorial: 310-858-7155
Subscriptions: 818-760-8983

PC Sources
Ziff-Davis Publishing Company
One Park Avenue
New York, NY 10016
Editorial: 212-503-3801
Subscriptions: 800-827-2078

Portable Computing
CurtCo Publishing
Warner Plaza V
21800 Oxnard Street
Suite 250
Woodland Hills, CA 91367
Editorial and subscriptions: 818-
593-6100.

Windows Sources
Ziff-Davis Publishing Company
One Park Avenue
New York, NY 10016
Editorial: 800-579-7889
Subscriptions: 800-365-3414

Windows User
Wandsworth Publishing, Inc.
25 West 39th Street
Suite 1103
New York, NY 10018
Editorial: 212-302-2626
Subscriptions: 800-627-9860

Windows Magazine
CMP Publications, Inc.
600 Community Dr.
Manhassett, NY 11030
Editorial: 516-562-7124
Subscriptions: 800-284-3584

Wireless
Probe Publishing Corp.
Three Wing Drive
Cedar Knolls, NJ 07927
Editorial and subscriptions: 201-285-1500.

WordPerfect for Windows
WPWin Magazine
270 West Center Street
Orem, UT 84057
Editorial: 801-226-5555
Subscriptions: 801-228-9626

WordPerfect the Magazine
WordPerfect Publishing
Corporation
270 West Center Street
Orem, UT 84057
Editorial: 801-226-5555
Subscriptions: 801-226-5556

Speeches and Seminars

Jeffrey J. Mayer would be delighted to speak at your next business meeting, conference, or convention. For date availability contact him at Mayer Enterprises, Inc.

Thoughts and Comments

If you would like to offer your thoughts or comments about this book, address them to the author at:

> Mayer Enterprises, Inc.
> 50 East Bellevue Place
> Chicago, IL 60611

INDEX OF SOFTWARE
MANUFACTURERS

Index of Software Manufacturers

ABC FlowCharter for Windows. Micrografx, 1303 Arapaho Road, Richardson, TX 75081; 214-234-1769. Suggested retail price: $495. See page 107.

Accu-Weather/Accu-Data. There is a subscription fee for subscribing to the Accu-Data database. For information contact an Accu-Weather Marketing representative at 814-234-9600, X400. See page 92.

Accu-Weather Forecaster. The Software Toolworks, 60 Leveroni Court, Novato, CA 94949; 800-234-3088. Suggested retail price: $24.95. See page 92.

Ace File. Ace Software Corporation, 1740 Technology Drive Suite 680, San Jose, CA 95110; 800-345-3223. Suggested retail price: $199. See page 65.

ACT! Symantec Corporation, 10201 Torre Avenue, Cupertino, CA 95014; 800-441-7234. Suggested retail price: $399. See page 60.

Address Express. CoStar Corporation, 100 Field Point Road, Greenwich, CT 06830; 800-426-9700. Suggested retail price: $795. See page 127.

Address Writer. CoStar Corporation, 100 Field Point Road, Greenwich, CT 06830; 800-426-9700. Suggested retail price: $399. See page 127.

America Online. America Online, Inc., 8619 Westwood Center Drive, Vienna, VA 22182; 800-827-6364. See page 87.

Approach. Approach Software Corporation, 311 Penobscot Drive, Redwood City, CA 94063; 800-277-7622. Suggested retail price: $299. See page 65.

Ascend. Franklin Quest Company, 220 West Parkway Boulevard, Salt Lake City, UT 84119; 800-654-1775. Suggested retail price: $149. See page 39.

AT&T EasyLink. AT&T EasyLink Services, 400 Interpace Parkway, Parsippany, NJ 07054; 800-435-7375. See page 90.

Bootcon. Modular Software Systems, 25826 104th Avenue SE, Kent, WA 98031; 800-438-3090. Suggested retail price: $79. See page 200.

By Design. Streetwise Software, 2210 Wilshire Boulevard, Santa Monica, CA 90403; 800-743-6765. Suggested retail price: $69. See page 124.

Calendar Creator Plus. Spinnaker Software Corporation, 201 Broadway, Cambridge, MA 02139; 800-851-2917. Suggested retail price: $59.95. See page 43.

Carbon Copy. Microcom, Inc., 500 River Ridge Drive, Norwood, MA 02062; 800-822-8224. Suggested retail price: $199. See page 94.

CardGrabber. Pacific Crest Technologies, 4000 MacArthur Boulevard, Newport Beach, CA 92660; 714-261-6444. Suggested retail price: $395. See page 79.

Central Point PC Tools. Central Point Software, 15220 NW Greenbrier Parkway, Suite 200, Beaverton, OR 97006; 800-365-8090. Suggested retail price: $179. See page 187.

Commence. Jensen-Jones, Inc., Parkway 109 Office Center, 328 Newman Springs Road, Red Bank, NJ 07701; 800-289-1548. Suggested retail price: $395. See page 60.

CompuServe. CompuServe Incorporated, 5000 Arlington Center Boulevard, P. O. Box 20212, Columbus, OH 43220, 800-368-3343. See page 87.

Computer Works. Software Marketing Corporation, 9830 South 51st Street Building A, Phoenix, AZ 85044; 800-545-6626. Suggested retail price: $79.95. See page 204.

CorelDRAW. Corel Corporation, 1600 Carling Avenue, Ottawa, Ontario, Canada K1Z8R7; 800-836-3729. Suggested retail price: $595. See page 117.

Corel Professional Photos. Corel Corporation, 1600 Carling Avenue, Ottawa, Ontario, Canada K1Z8R7; 800-772-6735. Suggested retail price: $49.95. See page 159.

Criterion Chairs. Steelcase Inc., Grand Rapids, MI 49501. Criterion chairs come with either a highback or a midback. The armrests are optional. For a catalog and a current price list call 800-333-9939. See page 213.

CypherScan. CypherTech, 250 Caribbean Drive, Sunnyvale, CA 94089; 408-734-8765. Suggested retail price: $395. See page 79.

DAZzle. Envelope Manager Software, 247 High Street, Palo Alto, CA 94301; 800-576-3279. Suggested retail price $39.95. See page 128.

DAZzle Designer. Envelope Manager Software, 247 High Street, Palo Alto, CA 94301; 800-576-3279. Suggested retail price $129.95. See page 128.

DAZzle Plus. Envelope Manager Software, 247 High Street, Palo Alto, CA 94301; 800-576-3279. Suggested retail price $79.95. See page 128.

Delphi. Delphi Internet Services Inc., 1030 Massachusetts Avenue, Cambridge, MA 02138; 800-491-3393. See page 87.

DeskMail. Western Union, Priority Services, One Lake Street, Upper Saddle River, NJ 07458; 800-336-3337. See page 91.

Desktop Projection and Cyclops. Proxima Corporation, 6610 Nancy Ridge Drive, San Diego, CA 92121. Proxima Corporation offers a complete line of LCD projection panels and the Cyclops interactive pointer system. Call 800-447-7694 for product information and a list of current prices. See page 145.

Desk Top Set. Okna Corporation, P. O. Box 522, Lyndhurst, NJ 07071; 800-765-5570. Suggested retail price: $195. See page 60.

DOS 6.0 includes a memory management feature called MemMaker. Microsoft Corporation, One Microsoft Way, Redmond, WA 98052; 800-426-9400. Suggested retail price: $129.95. See page 197.

DragonDictate. Dragon Systems, Inc., 320 Nevada Street, Newton, MA 02160; 800-825-5897. Suggested retail price: $4,995. See pages 151, 185, 221.

Dynodex. Portfolio Software, Inc., 10062 Miller Avenue, Cupertino, CA 95014; 800-729-3966. Suggested retail price: $89.95. The suggested retail price for **Dynopage** is $89.95. See page 56.

EasyFlow. HavenTree Software Limited, P. O. Box 470, Fineview, NY 13640; 800-267-0668. Suggested retail price: $280. See page 107.

Eclipse FAX. Phoenix Technology, Ltd., 33 West Monroe Street, Chicago, IL 60603; 800-452-0120. Suggested retail price: $129. See page 69.

Eclipse Find. Phoenix Technologies Ltd., 846 University Avenue, Norwood, MA 06062; 800-278-7197. Suggested retail price: $89.95. See page 184.

Envelope Manager. Envelope Manager Software, 247 High Street, Palo Alto, CA 94301; 800-576-3279. Suggested retail price $79.95. See page 130.

Envisions. Envisions Solutions Technology, Inc., 822 Mahler Road, Burlingame, CA 94010; 800-365-7226. Suggested retail price for black-and-white handheld scanners: $179. Suggested retail price for a color flatbed scanner: $899. See page 78.

ExecuVoice is bundled with Media Vision's Pro AudioStudio 16 sound card, their Pro Audio PowerPak, and their Pro 16 Multimedia System. See page 149.

Exercise Break. Hopkins Technology, 421 Hazel Lane, Hopkins, MN 55343; 800-397-9211. Suggested retail price $29.95. See page 226.

Expense It! On The Go Software, 4225 Executive Square, LaJolla, CA 92037; 619-558-4114. Suggested retail price: $129.99. See page 114.

Expert Mouse. Kensington Microware Limited, 2855 Campus Drive, San Mateo, CA 94403; 800-535-4242. Suggested retail price: $149.95. See page 219.

E-Z Track. E-Z Data, Inc., 533 S. Atlantic Boulevard, Monterey Park, CA 91754; 800-777-9188. Suggested retail price: $195. See page 60.

Facelift for Windows. Bitstream Inc., 215 First Street Cambridge, MA 02142; 800-522-3668. Suggested retail price: $99. See page 121.

Fastlynx. Rupp Technologies, 3228 E. Indian School Road, Phoenix, AZ 85018; 800-844-7775. Suggested retail price: $169.95. See page 95.

FastTrack Schedule. AEC Software, 22611 Markey Court, Sterling, VA 20166; 800-346-9413. Suggested retail price: $279. See page 102.

FAXGrabber. Calera Recognition Systems, 475 Potero Avenue, Sunnyvale, CA 94085; 800-422-5372. Suggested retail price: $89. See page 73.

FileMaker Pro. Claris Corporation, 5201 Patrick Henry Drive, Box 58168, Santa Clara, CA 95952; 800-544-8554. Suggested retail price: $129. See page 65.

FileRunner. MBS Technologies, Inc., 4017 Washington Road, McMurray, PA 15317; 800-867-8700. Suggested retail price: $99.95. See page 96.

FlowChart for Windows. Prisma Software, 401 Main Street, Cedar Falls, IA 50613; 800-437-3685. Suggested retail price: $89. See page 107.

Flow Charting 3. Patton & Patton Software Corporation, 485 Cochrane Circle, Morgan Hill, CA 95037; 408-778-6557. Suggested retail price: $250. See page 107.

Gantt Chart. Prisma Software Corporation, 2301 Clay Street, Cedar Falls, IA 50613; 800-437-2685. Suggested retail price: $89. See page 102.

GEnie. GE Information Services, 401 N. Washington Street, Rockville, MD 20850; 800-638-9636. See page 87.

Golden Retriever. Above Software, Inc., 2698 White Road, Suite 200, Irvine, CA 92714; 800-344-0116. Suggested retail price: $99.00 See page 183.

Hayes Modems. Hayes Microcomputer Products, Inc. P. O. Box 105203, Atlanta, GA 30348. Call 404-840-9200 for a catalog, price list, and the name of your nearest Hayes dealer. See page 84.

HealthDesk. HealthDesk Corporation, 1801 Fifth Street, Berkeley, CA 94701; 800-578-5767. Suggested retail price $99.95. See page 227.

Hewlett-Packard. P. O. Box 10301, Palo Alto, CA 94304; 800-752-0900. Suggested retail price for a black-and-white flatbed scanner: $879. See page 78.

HP 100LX. Hewlett-Packard, P. O. Box 10723, Portland, OR 97219; 800-443-1254. Suggested retail price: $749. See page 49.

Images. Image-X International, 5765 Thornwood Drive, Goleta, CA 93117; 805-946-3535. Suggested retail price for Images: $295. See page 74. (Mention this book and you can get Images for $99.)

Improv. Lotus Development Corporation, 55 Cambridge Parkway, Cambridge, MA 02142; 800-343-5414. Suggested retail price: $495. See page 134.

Info Select. Micro Logic Corporation, P. O. Box 70 Hackensack, NJ 07602; 800-342-5930. Suggested retail price: $149.95. See page 45.

ISYS. Odyssey Development, Inc., 650 South Cherry Street, Denver, CO 80222; 800-992-4797, Suggested retail price for the single user: $395; for three-station concurrent user: $795; five-station concurrent user: $1,295. See page 184.

Jumbo Tape Backup System. Colorado Memory Systems, Inc., 800 S. Taft Avenue, Loveland, CO 80537; 800-451-4523. Colorado Memory Systems makes many different sizes and types of tape drives. See page 189.

Kinesis Ergonomic Keyboard. Kinesis Corporation, 915 118th Avenue Southeast, Bellevue, WA 98005; 800-454-6374. Suggested retail price $390. See page 217.

LaserFiche. Compulink Management Center, Inc., 370 S. Crenshaw Boulevard, Torrance, CA 90503; 310-212-5465. Suggested retail price for the stand-alone version: $895. Suggested retail price for the network version depends upon the number of users. Five users: $4,995. Twenty users: $7,995. Fifty users: $18,995. One hundred users: $24,495. See page 81.

Lotus Organizer. Lotus Development Corporation, 55 Cambridge Parkway, Cambridge, MA 02142; 800-343-5414. Suggested retail price: $149. See page 36.

ManagePro. Avantos Performance Systems, Inc., 5900 Hollis Street, Emeryville, CA 94608; 800-282-6867. Suggested retail price: $395. See page 100.

Marquardt-Miniergo Keyboard. Marquardt Switches, 2711 Route 20 East, Cazenovia, NY 13035; 315-655-8050. Suggested retail price: $179. See page 217.

Maxtor Corporation makes a complete line of hard disk drives. Maxtor Corporation, 2190 Miller Drive, Longmont, CO 80501; 800-262-9867. See page 179.

MCI Mail. MCI International, 11330 19th Street NW, Washington, DC 20036; 800-444-6245. See page 90.

Meckler Corporation. 11 Ferry Lane West, Westport, CT 06880; 800-635-5537. See page 161.

Med$ure. Time Solutions, 45 Kellers Farm Road, Easton, CT 06612; 800-552-3302. Suggested retail price $69.95. See page 229.

MergeMaster. Stairway Software, 913 First Colonial Road, Virginia Beach, VA 23454; 800-782-4792. Suggested retail price: $79.95. See page 66.

Milestones, Etc. Kidasa Software, 1114 Lost Creek Boulevard, Austin, TX 78746; 800-765-0167. Suggested retail price: $189. See page 102.

Monologue 16 for Windows is bundled with Media Vision's Pro AudioStudio 16 sound card, their Pro Audio PowerPak, and their Pro 16 Multimedia System. See page 148.

Nanao USA Corporation. 23535 Telo Avenue, Torrance, CA 90505. Nanao makes a complete line of high- and ultrahigh-resolution color monitors from fifteen inches to twenty-one inches in size. For a catalog and a current price list call 800-800-5202. See page 215.

Norton Antivirus. Symantec Corporation, 10201 Torre Avenue, Cupertino, CA 95014; 800-441-7234. Suggested retail price: $129. See page 195.

Norton Backup. Symantec Corporation, 10201 Torre Avenue, Cupertino, CA 95014; 800-441-7234. Suggested retail price: $149. See page 187.

Norton Utilities. Symantec Corporation has incorporated disk caching in its Norton Utilities. Symantec Corporation, 10201 Torre Avenue, Cupertino, CA 95014; 800-441-7234. Suggested retail price: $179. See page 240. For Norton disk cache, see page 198.

ODIS. Image-X International, 5765 Thornwood Drive, Goleta, CA 93117; 805-946-3535. Suggested retail price for ODIS: $495. If you mention that you read about the product in this book, you can purchase ODIS for $295. If you need additional disk storage, floppy optical drives are available. See page 78.

Office Accelerator. Baseline Data Systems, Inc., 3625 Del Amo Boulevard, Suite 245, Torrance, CA 90503; 800-429-5325. Suggested retail price: $69.95. See page 42.

"1000 of the World's Greatest Sound Effects." InterActive Publishing Corporation, 300 Airport Executive Park, Spring Valley, NY 10977; 914-426-0400. Suggested retail price: $49.95. See page 160.

Optionist. Haven Tree Software, P. O. Box 470, Fineview, NY 13640; 800-267-0668. Suggested retail price: $299. See page 97.

Packrat 5.0. Polaris Software, 17150 Via Del Campo, Suite 307, San Diego, CA 62127; 800-722-5728. Suggested retail price: $395. See page 60.

Paper Direct. 205 Chubb Avenue, Lyndhurst, NJ 07071. For a catalog call 800-272-3777. See page 124.

pcAnywhere. Symantec Corporation, 10201 Torre Avenue, Cupertino, CA 95014; 800-441-7234. Suggested retail price: $199. See page 94.

Personal-E Mailbox. AmerCom Inc., P. O. Box 19868, Portland, OR 97280, 800-239-8295. Suggested retail price for a single user: $49; twin packs: $79; and six-packs: $129. See page 90.

Plantronics. 345 Encinal Street, Santa Cruz, CA 95060. For a catalog and a current price list call 800-426-5858. See page 223.

PrinterFax. Moonlight Computer Products, 10211 Pacific Mesa Boulevard, San Diego, CA 92121; 619-625-0300. Suggested retail price: $259. See page 74.

PrintQ. Software Directions, Inc., 1572 Sussex Turnpike, Randolph, NJ 07869; 800-346-7638. Suggested retail price: $149. See page 125.

Pro AudioStudio 16. Media Vision, Inc., 47300 Bayside Parkway, Fremont, CA 94538; 800-845-5870. Suggested retail price: $349. See page 146.

Prodigy. Prodigy Services Company, 445 Hamilton Avenue, White Plains, NY 10601; 800-776-3449. See page 87.

Pro MovieStudio. Media Vision, Inc., 47300 Bayside Parkway, Freemont CA 94538; 800-845-5879. Suggested retail price: $449. See page 167.

Project Scheduler. Scitor Corporation, 393 Vintage Park Drive, Foster City, CA 94404; 415-570-7700. Suggested retail price: $695. See page 102.

Pro 16 Multimedia System II. Media Vision, Inc., 47300 Bayside Parkway, Freemont, CA 94538; 800-845-5879. Suggested retail price: $1,195. See page 162.

QEMM-386. Quarterdeck Office Systems, 150 Pico Boulevard, Santa Monica, CA 90405; 800-354-3222. Suggested retail price: $99.95 See page 197.

QuickBooks. Intuit, P. O. Box 3014, Menlo Park, CA 94026; 800-624-6095. Suggested retail price: $139.95. See page 133.

Quicken. Intuit, P. O. Box 3014, menlo Park, CA 94026; 800-624-6095. Suggested retail price: $69.95. See page 131.

Ready, Aim, FILE! V Soft Development Corporation, 346 State Place, Escondido, CA 92029; 800-845-4843. Suggested retail price: $129.95 See page 183.

Recording Session is bundled with Media Vision's Pro AudioStudio 16 sound card, their Pro Audio PowerPak, and their Pro 16 Multimedia System. See page 153.

Santé. Hopkins Technology, 421 Hazel Lane, Hopkins, MN 55343; 800-397-9211. Suggested retail price $59.95. See page 230.

Sharkware, Harvey Mackay's System for Success. CogniTech Corporation, P. O. Box 500129, Atlanta, GA 31150; 800-947-5075. Suggested retail price: $129.95 See page 60.

Smartcom. Hayes Microcomputer Products, Inc. P. O. Box 105203, Atlanta, GA 30348. Call 404-840-9200 for a catalog, price list, and the name of your nearest Hayes dealer. See page 85.

Smart Label Printer Pro. Seiko Instruments USA Inc., 1130 Ringwood Court, San Jose, CA 95131; 800-888-0817. Suggested retail price: $299.95. See page 126.

Stacker. Stac Electronics, 5993 Avenida Encinas, Carlsbad, CA 92008, 800-522-7822. Suggested retail price: $139.95. See page 177.

Super PC-KWIK. PC-KWIK offers a disk caching program, Super PC-KWIK, and a companion product, PC-KWIK Power Pack, which has utilities that make your screen scroll faster, speed up your keyboard, and give you more control over your printing. PC-KWIK Corporation, 15100 SW Koll Parkway, Beaverton, OR 97006; 800-274-5945. Suggested retail price for Super PC-KWIK: $79.95. Suggested retail price for Power Pak: $129.95 See page 198.

Time Plus. Day Runner, Inc., 2750 West Moore Avenue, Fullerton, CA 92633; 800-232-9786. Suggested retail price: $60. See page 52.

Time$heet Professional. Timeslips Corporation, 239 Western Avenue, Essex, MA 01929; 800-285-0999. Suggested retail price: $199.95 See page 112.

Timeslips. Timeslips Corporation, 239 Western Avenue, Essex, MA 01929; 800-285-0999. Suggested retail price: $299.95 See page 110.

TrakMate: The Wristpad with the Trackball. Key Tronic, P. O. Box 14687, Spokane, WA 99214; 800-262-6006. Suggested retail price $149. See page 220.

TrueEffects for Windows. MicroLogic Software, 1351 Ocean Avenue, Emmeryville, CA 94608; 800-888-9078. Suggested retail price: $59.95. See page 121.

UnInstaller. MicroHelp, Inc., 439 Shallowford Industrial Parkway, Marietta, GA 30066; 800-922-3383. Suggested retail price: $79. See page 175.

Values Quest. Franklin Quest Company, 220 West Parkway Boulevard, Salt Lake City, UT 84119; 800-654-1775. Suggested retail price: $49.95. See page 58.

Visio. Shapeware Corporation, 1601 Fifth Avenue, Seattle, WA 98101; 800-446-3335. Suggested retail price: $299. See page 116.

Windows. Microsoft Corporation, One Microsoft Way, Redmond, WA 98052; 800-426-9400. Suggested retail price: $149.95. See page 20. For windows disk cache, see page 198.

Windows Express. hDC Computer Corporation, 6742 185th Avenue NE, Redmond, WA 98052; 800-321-4606. Suggested retail price: $99.95. See page 183.

Windows OrgChart. Micrografx, Inc., 1303 Arapaho Road, Richardson, TX 75081; 800-733-3729. Suggested retail price: $149. See page 109.

Winfax Pro. Delrina Technology Inc., 6830 Via Del Oro, San Jose, CA 95119; 800-268-6082. Suggested retail price: $129. See page 69.

Winfo. Win Ware Inc., 4665 Lower Roswell Road, Marietta, GA 30068; 800-336-5985. Suggested retail price: $49.95. See page 59.

WordPerfect InForms. WordPerfect Corporation, 1555 N. Technology Way, Orem, UT 84057; 800-451-5151. The cost of InForms depends upon the number of users on your network. The suggested retail price for the stand-alone version is $495. See page 115.

WordPerfect Office 4.0. WordPerfect Corporation, 1555 N. Technology Way, Orem, UT 84057; 800-451-5151. The suggested retail price for the administration and server package is $295, and the suggested retail price for a client pack with five mailbox licenses is $495. Licenses for additional users are available. See page 47.

WordPerfect Office 3.1. WordPerfect Corporation, 1555 N. Technology Way, Orem, UT 84057; 800-451-5151. Suggested retail price: $149. See page 53.

WordPerfect Presentations. WordPerfect Corporation, 1555 N. Technology Way, Orem, UT 84057, 800-451-5151. Suggested retail price: $495. See page 140.

WordPerfect 6.0. WordPerfect Corporation, 1555 N. Technology Way, Orem, UT 84957; 800-451-5151. Suggested retail price: $495. See page 201.

WordScan Plus. Calera Recognition Systems, 475 Potero Avenue, Sunnyvale, CA 94085; 800-422-5372. Suggested retail price: $295. See page 80.

YourWay. Prisma Software Corporation, 2301 Clay Street, Cedar Falls, IA 50613; 800-437-2685. Suggested retail price: $99. See page 39.